You Break It, You Buy It

Owning the Life Behind the Broken Reflection

Foreword by Diana Festejo

LEGACY PLACE
—SOCIETY—

PEACEMAN
Consulting

Peaceman Publishing

2018

Copyright © 2018 by Dean R. Young

First Printing: 2018

ISBN: 978-1-387-43130-4

Peaceman Publishing

Strathmore, Alberta, Canada

www.peaceman.ca

Dedication

To all my brother and sister first responders

Suffering for being the good guys

&

To my wife and children

Who still help fight off the chickens

(see Chapter 5)

Acknowledgements

Many people have contributed to my experiences and, in turn, contributed to the content of this book. It is amazing when I look back to see how each and every co-worker, employer, mentor, professor, supporter and detractor shaped me into the person I am today. I would like to mention a few:

- My friends, colleagues, and students over the years have very much helped me see me for who I truly am, modelled behaviours that I saw to be valuable enough to emulate, and for contributing to the joy I felt when I was in their company.

- I.M., J.F., and G.B., each of whose experiences impacted me profoundly, both professionally and personally. You have helped put me on the path of my own pursuit of peacefulness and mindfulness. Each of you have shown me how deep and dark of which we as professional first responders are capable, and for demonstrating how successfully we as professional first responders can rise out of the pit of despair, and I thank you for it.

- Aziz Khadem and Sue Evans, each of whom impacted me profoundly, both professionally and personally. You have provided me with mentorship, camaraderie, laughs, and the opportunity to prove myself in the absence of anything other than passion for the law enforcement and security fields. Each of you contributed to my professionalism and leadership and I thank you for it.

Table of Contents

Foreword

As a registered charity based in Alberta, Legacy Place Society is uniquely positioned with a specific focus dedicated to providing confidential and collaborative resources to the individuals and families of first responders and military personnel.

You will see that in *You Break It, You Buy It*, Dean Young shares numerous lived experiences from himself and fellow colleagues. These lived experiences and personal stories of impact on mental wellbeing and on their families, are real realities many face. They, along with the millions of First Responders and Military Personnel around the world, endure and courageously navigate in and around dangerous and incredibly unique situations associated with their professions. In their lines of work, each day brings challenging realities with which to cope, including the many split-second and long-term decisions that decide the safety, law and order, and lifesaving with the calls that come in.

Over the years, the harm associated to smoking, alcohol, obesity are some examples of where health issues have become a need to be addressed. Today's airwaves speak to mental health including addictions, suicide, stigma and stories of heartache. These stories tend to encompass celebrities, athletes and the general public. It is difficult when one of these stories involves someone from the first responder or military membership that results in tragedy due to line of duty death or suicide. Take into consideration all of this, and then include shift work, long hours and changes in their own personal lives with marriage, kids, health, aging parents and economic circumstances. An unwanted brown envelope of divorce papers, shame and guilt of financial difficulties or domestic abuse, secrets to alcohol addictions, depression, anxiety can all be hard to live with. Throw in there balancing a demanding shift work life and other aspects of life in general with special needs, a medical crisis and such. It can throw us into catastrophic grief.

The media sound bites do not tell the full story and sometimes not with full accuracy. Social media feeds typically present interpretations on situations in rapid, incomplete and distasteful response. The Canadian flag flying at half mast and the black thin line on the membership crest is becoming more frequent and, once again, tragically brings together the somber faces of surviving colleagues and family.

Since the late 1990s, there have been many first responder suicides in Alberta—in review of what was happening, it has become clear that peer support and attention to the mental health arena was, and still is, needed. It was becoming more evident that coping behaviour were contributing to the lack of wellbeing, destruction of marriages and family relationships, and ultimately the individual. Such maladaptive coping mechanisms included excess drinking, risky behaviour, sleeping in cars, and couch surfing. Sometimes escalated anger or friendship with Jack Daniels have contributed to more struggles.

So how does Legacy Place Society fit into this? As so many in this audience can relate, it can be extremely difficult to drop the shifts activities at the door and slide into a family routine, to have those carefully crafted conversations at the dinner table with innocent ears wide open, or have the pillow talk with your spouse/partner. What do you say or not say? Sometimes the stressors catch up and the structure of life at home is compromised.

Primarily Legacy Society is a home away from home providing short term support that can help the individual get rest, pull thoughts into perspective and continue the work schedule. Currently in Calgary, Red Deer and Edmonton, we have houses that provide short term confidential support to Peace Officers/ Police, Fire, EMS, 911 communications operators and military families—a recent example: thirty-three thousand night-stays in a single year of operation; twenty-one hundred clients just for house use alone. To date, these three houses have supported over twenty-one hundred clients and over thirty-three thousand overnight stays.

Average stay varies, but sometimes the stay is just a few days, and in some cases, up to a few months—each case is assessed on its own merit. Medical concerns including trauma, post-traumatic stress, operational or occupational stress injuries, cancer, and/or relationships that are struggling—all stuff that is personal. This accommodation piece is critical and is an available resource to access.

The adversarial challenges of noise, rush-rush, and crowds are tough especially when treatment is being sought out for post-traumatic stress. A common comment from our clients is about how quiet it is—providing them with the opportunity to catch up on sleep—it provides rest and clarity.

Legacy Place Society works beyond individual psychological/medical situations but also when marriages are slipping sideways; there is a process in place to either re-establish the relationship or support the member when it is dissolving. In an extremely tight economic environment, it can be difficult to sign anything less than a six month or one-year lease. Sometimes we get calls, a first responder has their bags at the door, and have been told to get it together.

Our mission and values also include programs involving family camps, mission trips, first responder and military personnel psychological wellness and suicide awareness conferences. We get asked which membership utilizes us the most. We are not in any position to suggest one membership is more fit or healthy than the other and we are not out there showing our face in the media suggesting that PTSD or lack of resources is the issue. There are numerous issues. Focus, having the mindset of being pro-active, intentional budgets being in place and people resources are key within all membership.

We collaborate because when membership and individuals converge together, to learn from each other, there is power and hope. We are excited to see activities associated to the support of better understanding of mental health and wellness, peer support and chaplaincy support, being incorporated within. Much like we do with physical exercise, encouraging ways towards self-care, and emotional wellness, engage in peer support opportunities, access to employee assistance programs, we encourage the reader to consider participating in any of our workshops or mission trips, and involve themselves in these types of celebratory events.

Many organizations, such as Legacy Place Society, are working hard to provide understanding and support, life enrichment and legacies of hope. It is a shared responsibility and requires balance.

Why am I telling you this—it is… because Legacy has navigated through some extremely difficult years of healing and setbacks, triggers and emotions that still linger today with many who have stepped forward to access our programs. This includes shame, disappointment, fear, rejection, financial ruin… to just mention a few. Vicarious trauma, moral injury, grief, and compassion fatigue are real and very common simply due to the carnage our men and women have faced and continue to face today. Long after the experience has ended.

Sometimes it is hard to know what is harder: learning about the situation an individual or family is going through or hearing that the person has no one to lean on as an emergency contact or, worse yet, is uncertain to whom to turn. "How about your mom or dad, a co-worker, sibling, friend?" "No, I don't want them to know, (or…) we are estranged, (or…) they are hurting enough themselves, (or…) I don't trust anyone or think that anyone will understand what I'm going through.

It's terrifying to talk about suicide! Still fresh in our organization's past, a call came through from one of the policing agencies, demanding to know where our house was, because an individual did not have a court case go in their favour and co-workers were concerned for his wellbeing as he had not checked in with someone a couple hours later. Long story short—the police accessed the home and found one of our clients, one of their co-workers, self-injured on the kitchen floor. No one thought he would make it, but he did. We took him back in a few weeks later to assist in additional transition with his journey. Today he is thriving.

This past year Legacy Place Society had twenty-seven situations that were suicidal in nature. Some harmful items meant to cause personal harm have been surrendered to us, and some clients have been successfully transitioned out of exceptional out-treatment addiction programs.

Fear and dread of perhaps a bleak future can color our thinking until we can see another way out. Should we be furious because it's happened? Who do we get angry at? Who and what do we blame? So, we extend our offer of talking more openly about the toxic whisper of suicide, depression and the challenges affecting first responders and military personnel. We must get better at disclosing it, give permission to talking about it, encourage the seeking of help, and continuing to offer hope to each other beyond the destructive companions of fear.

When we bring on the compelling stories of resiliency and lived experience we find a common thread: epic feats of resiliency, perseverance, endurance and courage. We all are a legacy of hope to each other, our children, our spouses, family and friends... Today and each day going forward let our conversations connect, communicate and care—with each other and with ourselves.

You will see by the experiences contained in this book that it is critical that we lead by example—let us be the ones who reach out to our peers, who speak up, listen, remove the stigma and make a difference for someone around you who may be suffering.

Diana Festejo
Executive Director
Legacy Place Society

For more information about Legacy Place Society:
www.legacyplacesociety.com
info@legacyplacesociety.com http://www.facebook.com/legacyplacesociety/

Preface

I began this book, in so many different forms, oh so many years ago, and it's gone from a book on leadership, a life's lessons learned book, incorporating leadership, integrity, positivity, continuous learning and stress and mental health to this. During that time, my own stresses and mental health issues came home to roost, and I took an interest in operational stress injuries. The three friends, named in this book's acknowledgements section, provided the guidance for me to begin to accept and explore my own issues resulting from a life spent in the protective services and first responder worlds.

Writing this book has been the culmination of a life lived and lessons learned. I have struggled with common challenges we all face, both early in life and later into middle age. Along the way, I encountered opportunities to learn about myself, people around me and the world around me. And in doing so, aside from a few… setbacks…, I took control of my life and my self, with the ultimate effect of gaining control over my destiny. My years of emergency response situations in which I encountered people suffering emotional anguish, horrific injuries, people facing their own deaths, and ultimately me facing death, seeing it, touching it have created a sense of well worn. I believed that I was handling all this trauma well, but I was wrong. Eventually, the stress took control of my life and my self, with the ultimate effect of gaining control over my destiny. Thanks to my friends and family, starting with my wife when she ratted me out to my doctor, I have been on a journey of self exploration and learning how to take back my mind and my life before I become irreparably broken.

Brian Willis, a world-renowned police trainer, holds forth his W.I.N approach to life and work. W.I.N stands for What's Important Now. He teaches that, whenever we make decisions, the first and most important question to ask ourselves is "what's important now". I have identified my need and readiness to work on healing myself. As I write and facilitate workshops in all industries, I want people to understand that change and self-improvement is possible, and I firmly believe that anyone can change. That said, it isn't easy, and it doesn't happen overnight. This isn't some new age caressing of crystals and meditation approach, nor is this approach that of sitting around a fire, holding hands and singing campfire songs and sharing deep dark secrets. I can change, and it has improved my conditions greatly, providing the benefits not only to me, but to all those my life touches. It's been quite the journey so far… it's hard… but I know I'm not having to do it alone. Here's the story of my journey.

A brief note on gender in this book…I wish to acknowledge the role that women play in the first responder services. It is both my thought and experience that women are just as capable players in the emergency services industry. That said, I will be using the masculine pronoun in general throughout this book in the interest of convenience and reading ease, and in no way am I portraying a marginalized role of women as first responders. "He", "him", and "his" could just as readily be "she", "her" and "hers".

A brief note on the science in this book... just an acknowledgement that I am not a scientist, a doctor, a psychologist, or any other -ologist. I know that what I have written is so much a simplification of the true biology and psychology involved with stress and mental health issues. I am including what I feel is important to give the reader a basic picture of the body and brain and its relation to behaviour.

Finally, please be aware that there very well may be content in this book that may act as triggers for the reader. I want to explicitly state that you need to care for yourself and keep yourself safe if that happens. Names in this book have been changed, not because the contributors wished anonymity, but because of my respect for their privacy.

Come... take my hand and I'll take you down into the pit and we'll re-emerge together...

CHAPTER 1

Irreparably Broken: The Tragic Reality

The unfortunate reality is that, gone untreated or unsuccessfully treated, operational stress disorders can and does lead to the breaking of our brothers and sisters. I call these men and women irreparably broken since they, unlike those of us who are strictly gently used or well worn, are broken beyond repair. Once you are dead, you cannot fix anything.

According to the Tema Conter Memorial Trust (2017)[1], a hub for research and education for the first responders serving in Canada's public safety organizations, during the years between 2014 to the end of 2017, we have lost no less than one hundred and seventy-one first responders by their own hands: twenty-seven in 2014, fifty-one in 2015, forty-eight in 2016 and forty-five in 2017. These are the numbers of first responder deaths that were determined to be and recorded as suicide. This does not account for the deaths deemed accidental, or unknown causes, or erroneously deemed natural causes. One factor that does not usually get put into these statistics are those people who succumbed to the various diseases attributed to physiological breakdown of the body from being marinated in stress chemicals for so many years.

Another factor of which we need to be cognisant is just like any other suicide is the people left behind. We all hear of the pain of those close to someone who fell victim to their demons, first responder or otherwise. I write about the impacts of suicide on survivors; however, I am not writing about the inevitable pain that is left in the wake of these tragedies. The point I want to make clear here is that

---

[1] www.tema.ca

the number of first responders who are taking their own lives is not dropping. What I fear is illustrated in the following story.

In January of 2015, a paramedic died took his own life after struggling with operational stress injuries. Less than a month later, the local newspaper published a letter received by an anonymous first responder. This letter was a very bitter letter, full of condemnation of the local EMS and health authorities for the writer's perceived lack of support, and evokes a picture of a person who is utterly devoid of hope. Here is an excerpt of the letter published online:

> *"I will live with my depression and other mental illness until the day I die, I will forever be plagued by the thoughts that I should have done my wife and kids a favour and went out like [paramedic] did long ago instead of subjecting them to a life lived with a person who no longer has emotion happy or sad thanks to depression and or the drugs that treat it. I will continue to feel a bit of jealousy each time a news story airs of a first responder who has committed suicide or was killed in the line of duty, and I'll continue to wish that I too could have been killed in the line of duty, so my family would have the memory of all the uniforms at my funeral and they could be proud of how I left earth."—February 2015*

My concern will always be this: is this letter indicative of the thoughts and feelings of our current first responders? It certainly is not for me; however, much of this bitterness, feeling of abandonment and utter failure to receive help is evident in the stories provided by John and Ian. This letter, and the underlying mental processes presents a very scary situation. The concept of copycat as it pertains to the phenomenon of suicide is always a disturbing trend, as we see people identifying with the suicide strictly because of some small perceived shared quality. Can this become an issue in our first responder communities? I invite you to return to the quoted section of the letter and dissect the wording. These are my concerns:

> *"<u>I will live with my depression and other mental illness until the day I die</u>, I will forever be plagued by the thoughts <u>that I should have done my wife and kids a favour and went out</u> like [paramedic] did long ago <u>instead of subjecting them to a life</u> lived with a person who no longer has emotion happy or sad thanks to depression and or the drugs that treat it. I will continue to feel <u>a bit of jealousy each time a news story airs of</u>*

a first responder who has committed suicide or was killed in the line of duty, and I'll continue to wish that I too could have been killed in the line of duty, so my family would have the memory of all the uniforms at my funeral and they could be proud of how I left earth."—February 2015

I find it disturbing that he felt that he is a plague to his family, and feels like he should do his wife and kids a favour and take his own life. He also apparently feels that his life with mental illness would somehow punish his family. All of that said, the real red flag for me is that he feels jealous of first responders who die, and that he wishes to die in the line of duty, and that he feels his family would be proud of his death.

I used to say to my wife that, if I had to die, I wanted to go out with a flag on my coffin. A very insensitive thing to say to my spouse for sure. I never really considered how such things sounded. The writer of this letter is obviously not just making absent minded quips; it is obvious to me that there is such pain and despair, and he means all that is written in that letter. As far as I am concerned, this is a suicide note. It may not occur today, tomorrow, next week, next month or even next year… but it will happen if something does not intervene in his path. According to the World Health Organization[2],

> *"Survivors are those who have lost someone to suicide. This could include immediate family members, close friends, co-workers or classmates. Reaching out to this vulnerable group is crucial, as they can be prone to depression and suicidal behaviours. This process, known as post-vention not only offers timely support to the bereaved but also becomes a method of suicide prevention in itself."*

It really seems to be that this letter writer exemplifies the need to intervene when someone is hurting, is despondent and admires colleagues who have chosen to take their own lives. In the case of Ian, we see the impact of the very same environment as the anonymous letter writer; however, in the case of John, we see the impact of being embraced by those who are in a position to intervene on the behalf of our suffering. I, too, am very fortunate to be surrounded by supportive colleagues, family, friends, and professional expertise. We'll discuss support more in "Nailing Down the Rug" chapter.

Beyond the cold statistics of first responder suicides, I want to discuss those left behind. For those who give in to the demons, the pain and suffering has ended. But what of those left behind to live with the loss. I do not know if surviving a loved one's suicide is any different that surviving the premature

---

[2] World Health Organization (2012). "Public Health Action for the prevention of Suicide: A Framework"

natural death, but as far as our discussion here is concerned, pain is pain and loss is loss, and unfair is unfair.

I've been fortunate that I have had very little experience in death and loss, and even less with suicide, short of walking into a former roommate's failed attempt. What I do have experience with is the most profound experience with personal loss to date. I was not very close to my grandparents; both of my grandfathers passed away when I was a young child. And my parents are still living. This is not to say that I have not been faced with death. My brother's best friend was accidentally killed in a motor vehicle collision. I knew this kid personally and it was difficult to manage, as I was only fifteen. I've attended funerals for colleagues, men and women who do what I do, and have died in the line of duty. As any who have attended such memorials, these are very difficult to attend.

Just prior to my wife outing me to my doctor about my issues, her mother, Darlene, contracted stage four lung cancer. For those, like me, who have never had to learn about the intricacies of cancer, stage four is virtually incurable and was the case with Darlene. As my wife is probably going to read this, I am not going to blather on about the science. If you wish to learn about it, there are plenty of cold facts on the Internet

I must admit that I struggle myself having to face the loss of my second mom. Our history is probably the typical one, but over the years, that relationship had grown to be one of love and value. I find myself thinking that I was not ready to let her go. But it was not up to us. That card had been played. My point, I guess, is to value the time we have with our brothers and sisters in the first responder family. I will not get too cheesy here, and I know that any of us can go at any time, but what's stopping us from taking time throughout the day to appreciate that which we value the most? We complain about our daily trials, but do we take any time to at least reflect on what we have won in life? I am. And topping that list is my family. I am grateful that my parents are still there for me, both in life and spirit. I am grateful that my wife and children have such an immensely close relationship with me. I always took it for granted that they always will be here, and I have always been able to put on my uniform and leave for work with the "It will not happen to me because I am cautious." I could not leave them every day if I focused on "Well, this might be my last day." But I think about them every day, and in every situation that might be a little hinkey while on the job. As part of my ongoing exploration into myself, this has become a major motivation for me to survive, both physically and emotionally.

It makes me that much more aware of life… mine… theirs'… and everyone around me. All I am suggesting right now is that perhaps we could all use a little thought toward those who we love and cherish. I know I am.

Although I will write more about chronic stress in a later chapter, I want to include here that chronic stress is a killer. My therapist put it succinctly: the number one killer that is never put on a death certificate is stress, especially the chronic kind. The body cannot sustain health when being constantly picked by stress hormones. This kills more first responders than suicide; however, as I hope to show, chronic stress can be alleviated by choice. If you choose to continue accumulating operational stress without finding real vents and coping strategies, is it akin to suicide? This is a question to which you should give significant thought. It is amazing that one cannot see the forest through the trees. I have spent the better part of twenty years learning all the intricacies of stress on the body and mind and yet not capable of applying them to one's self.

CHAPTER 2

Gently Used to Well Worn: The Story of This Guy

Introduction to the concept of the continuum of Gently Used to Well Worn and, tragically, to Irreparably Broken. We all hear of our fallen brothers and sisters at their own hands. These irreparably broken members are what we are fighting to prevent. The aim of this presentation is to explore how we can either remain near the Gently Used end or reduce our operational stress injuries to such a degree that irreparableness does not describe our brokenness.

When I finally had the opportunity to really contemplate first my symptoms, then my doctor's opinions about my condition, then the workers compensation authority psychologist's opinion during my assessment, then the psychiatrist that I was sent to (who confirmed the psychologist's findings), and finally my own chosen psychologist, it became very apparent that I had suffered from depression and anxiety since childhood. In retrospect, I considered how, when I was sixteen and my brother's best friend was killed during a bicycle collision, I first started suffering from intense migraines. All the doctors I had seen, including a neurologist, all agreed that the migraines were stress induced. These migraines were debilitating, causing altered states of consciousness and hemispheric paralysis… I got goofy and went physically numb on one side every time. I continue to suffer from migraines even to today, but they definitely do not compare to those when I was younger.

A note about insomnia. This is one of the pre-existing conditions that I have suffered from since I can remember. I always found myself reading into the wee hours, and then struggling to wake up in the morning. During my last summer in university, I lived in residence. I was one of the founding members of the Insomniac's Club for our floor. I just always had a very hard time falling asleep. One of the main aggravators of insomnia is the brain that just will not shut up. Thought suppression has been proven to not only not work, but has an ironic effect in that it compels you to think more on that very thought. I had this very badly. I found that the only way to combat this (and not always successfully) was working night shifts. I found I was better able to sleep during the day because by they my exhaustion and circadian rhymes finally jibed and would put me out. The unfair part of this was that it made me miserable, and just compounding my relationship issues with my wife.

Oh, and I always new that I was going to be a cop. And then a psychologist... that was the dream, anyway. But cop first! When I went off to university, I recall that I experienced many depressive episodes and more of a sense of isolation. I spent all my preteen and teen years a part of a significantly large social group of friends. Truly, the only drawback of this was that I never really learned how to make friends. I always met new people as they entered the group; I was secure in the sense that I could be myself and not having to work about impression management. However, I found when I went off to university, I had absolutely no relationship building skills, and I suffered for it. The point isn't that I can't make friends to save my life, I no longer had the support of friends, let alone family. You see, I chose not to go to a university that all my friends were attending. I found myself drinking too much, but then once again isolating myself. When I went out, I drank to have fun, then withdrew again. The binge partying lasted only a few months, and then I withdrew from most of life. Around this same time, I walked into my roommate's attempted suicide. Funny, but at the time, it just seemed like no big deal.

Eventually, my absentee rate went through the roof, I wasn't completing assignments, and my marks declined. I remember a period in my second year that I rarely even got out of bed. The long-term result of these missed classes was my first exposure to consequences. I came very close to being expelled. And still it never clicked that I was suffering from depression, despite having all the symptoms (I know, hindsight is 20/20). Fortunately, at the time, I was able to get to the point where at least I was cognisant of how to keep my head above the academic waters to graduate. It became very evident after the fact that I still lived with depression, and periodically dipped into the depths. There was a fair bit of time that I sat in my apartment and watched old TV shows and stuffed my face with Haagan Das®.

Upon graduation, I started work in the security industry to get some, what I thought would be, valuable work-related experience. Unfortunately, the experience I got was less than valuable, and more so just downright unethical. But that's for another book. What those experiences did introduce for the first time in my life was absolute dissatisfaction with the workplace. Leaders who were not good leaders, managers who were not good managers, and coworkers who were not good coworkers. Although I do not recall suffering any traumas during this time, I believe that the anxiety that was buried in the mine had its fuse lit. Most of my work life has been very rife with anxiety, not from the job itself, but the environment in which those jobs took place. There are just way too many examples; suffice it to say, I am not surprised that the anxiety was now coming to the forefront of my life. However, the sacrifice had to be made if I was to develop myself into the perfect police applicant.

I went on like this for years, especially because most of my jobs were night shift and evenings, so I really had no room for a social life, and I was too anxious to go out and find friends. I recall a conversation I had with myself (this will be a recurring theme), in that I told myself that once I have a day job, I would go out into the world and find a friend. I was probably just humouring myself. It finally did come to pass that I was working during the day. And it also came to pass that I got a call last minute from an acquaintance's girlfriend informing me that she had arranged a surprise birthday party for him, and she forgot to call me. As if it was just yesterday, I can still hear myself whining to myself:

> *"Meh... I'm not going to know anyone there (and you know how shy I am) ... and I just started growing my goatee back again and it's still in that cheesy porn stage... blah... blah... blah... I don't wanna go..."*

And then I retorted:

> *"Look here, you! You said that if you ever got a day job, you'd get a life. Well, here's the opportunity. So get your poop in a group and hit the road!"*

Stupid me... telling me what to do...

So off I went... and I was right... didn't know a single soul in the place. Would you like to hear something funny, though? I met my wife that night... and the rest is a whirlwind romance story! Well, that is until another chicken came home to roost. I didn't know it at the time, but my defense mechanisms were about to be challenged. The introduction of the relationship dynamic changed how effectively I would be able to manage conflict, and I found myself struggling... and failing... to manage my anxiety and depression. My inability to cope almost cost me my marriage, and finally demonstrated how utterly cancerous self talk can be. I will talk more about the derailing nature of self talk later in this book.

On top of all this conflict in my life, I started applying for police departments. Holy cow, did I not know what I was buying into there. The first few deferrals I understood. Inadequate physical fitness and nervousness in interviews cost me a few, but as I got more comfortable, I felt I was offering a very solid candidate. As there are so very many examples of how interactions with various police recruiting services had, and still have, scarred me, I'll just say that stress, self-doubt and frustration became the standard applicant process for me, as my hopes began to dwindle. However, at the point of joining the fire department (thinking this experience would help for my policing aspirations), I was not yet disillusioned as I will was to become later in life. I eventually forayed into the land of the first responder, joining my local fire department as a volunteer. Once the novelty wore off of wearing the bunker gear, waiting for the radio to tone me out, and driving a vehicle with lights and sirens, I started to focus on the meat of the job. I found I didn't care as much for the fire side of things, as I did handling the medical and rescue side of it. I had been a first aid instructor for a few years and enjoyed that very much.

My first memorable call was for a three-year-old whose arm was snagged by the auger mechanism in an industrial chicken feed apparatus. His arm was broken and had a significant long and deep laceration to the arm, and was contaminated with the chicken feed. This was the first time, also, that I saw STARS (Shock Trauma Air Rescue Services) air ambulance up close. At the time, my oldest daughter was around that very age. In retrospect, I do not recall that event having any real impact at the time. Thankfully, the little guy recovered from his injuries.

I went on a few other calls, including my first fatality (an impaired driver in a single vehicle collision). These calls I typically, being a rookie, took on the more menial roles, such as traffic control. However, the real eye opener for me was my second most memorable call. I just happened to be home that day because I worked shift-work, and this was my regular day off. The tones went off at around noon, so not a lot of members available, or even in town at the time. I made my way to the fire hall and found that I was the first responder. As we do not attend calls alone, I waited for other members to arrive, having prepared our rescue unit for departure. Of course, it is difficult to sit and wait when you know the scene is just sitting there waiting. Once other members arrived, we took off to the scene.

It appears that a vehicle traveling west on the highway and was approaching the creek that flowed under the highway. This driver reported that, as he entered the highway shortly before the event, there was no oncoming traffic. He then reported that, suddenly, this other vehicle was right behind him, almost out of nowhere. When the vehicle began to pass, it was driven into the driver's blind

spot and never passed. The driver stated that he had looked into his side mirror and observed the vehicle tumbling in the ditch, where it came to rest on its roof.

The vehicle had had four occupants, one of which was ejected and came to rest in a small slough approximately thirty metres from the vehicle. As it turns out, apparently the driver was traveling at excessive speeds, and when he left the lane to pass, he lost control of the vehicle and struck the guard rail. The vehicle left the road and crossed the creek, hitting the bank on the opposite side of the creek, and began to roll. It was during this rolling that the rear passenger was ejected (likely through the rear window).

Upon arrival, as I took in the scene, I observed the vehicle on its roof in a field, and two people doing CPR on a body quite some distance from the subject vehicle. I took the automated external defibrillator with me and hurried to the CPR scene, all the while listening to cries and screams coming from inside the vehicle. If you have been in the first responder industry, you will understand the tunnel vision often experienced in high stress situations. I had said blinders, and did not realize that I ran through a barbed wire fence that was snarled from the vehicle tumbling through.

As I arrived at the CPR site, one of the bystanders indicated that he was a volunteer firefighter from another municipality. I cleared the bystanders, assessed the casualty's pulse, found none and ensured the bystanders were capable to continuing CPR, then returned to the overturned vehicle. This, by the way, was the very first time I had physical contact with a deceased person.

As I began to assist the team at the vehicle, I discovered that there were three occupants in the vehicle. The driver was semi-conscious, the front passenger was unconscious, and the rear passenger was fully conscious and required extraction.

I was part of the team that extricated the driver, who had suffered head and spinal injuries, and had a fractured femur (the bone of the thigh). Having been a first aid instructor, I knew that fractured femurs can be a fatal injury if not stabilized effectively, and again, for the first time, I held and supported gently the thigh of

the driver as he was removed from the vehicle. In the meantime, STARS had arrived and was waiting for the patients.

Meanwhile, another team was working on removing the front passenger, who was in a position that made cutting away the door very difficult. However, the members were successful, and both patients were loaded into the air ambulance and taken from the scene. During this phase of the rescue, the rear passenger continued to scream and flail in the back seat. Once the others were extricated, attention was turned to removing this man. As it turns out, during the rolling of the vehicle, his foot somehow became trapped above the passenger's seat headrest when the roof collapsed.

To add injury to insult, his foot was twisted at a one-eighty angle. Remember, he's been conscious the entire time, and this would have been an incredibly painful condition. Trying to calm him down and to limit his movement to prevent further injury was a task in itself. It seemed that the extrication team was having difficulty moving the roof, and there was some talk from a paramedic that there may be the need for a field surgeon. Fortunately, this was ultimately not required, as soon thereafter, the foot came loose, and the patient was transported by STARS, which had the time to deliver the original two patients and to return to the scene.

During the inevitable debrief, I was informed that the deceased was a youth, and was the only occupant not wearing a seatbelt. I am not going to jump on a soapbox about the necessity of seat-belts, so you can take away from this story whatever message you care to take. It was also the first time I second-guessed my actions on a scene. I voiced my concerns about not trying the AED on the patient, of course forgetting that AED's do nothing for trauma casualties, and was informed that the spine of the youth had become detached from the brain stem, and there was no hope of revival, regardless of intervention. It was a difficult call to process and put it away due to the fact that I had to drive by the location everyday as I traveled into work, or anywhere else for that matter. Unbeknownst to me, this was yet another trauma stacked up on the others to date.

The third most memorable call was that of a stroke casualty in the town that I lived. The tones went off just as I had gone to bed. Waking up when tones go just wreaks havoc on the system, as it is like waking up because someone threw a bucket of ice water on you. Or at least that was how it was for me. Instant adrenaline, going from zero to one hundred in a half-second. Also, not healthy. I ended up driving passed the scene as we were required by policy to attend the hall and go with the rest of the responders. I recall being first on scene to a bi-level house, you know… open the door, immediate stairs up and down. I had the AED with me, and an oxygen rig. I opened the door and announced myself. The kitchen was pure chaos… crying, panic, etc. I announced again, and someone came to the top of the stairs and pointed down the upstairs hallway. As I knew my partner was nearby, I entered the house, went up the stairs and started to walk down the hall. As it turns out, the casualty was in the master bedroom at the end of the hall. I walked into the bedroom (not recalling seeing anyone in the room), and went into the *en suite* bathroom and found the casualty lying naked on the floor.

Just for a back-story, apparently the casualty, the husband and father of four or five children, had gone to have a shower. Mom heard a thump and asked teen son to investigate. Son found dad on the floor, suffering from a massive stroke. Mom dialled 9-1-1 and was shouting directions for CPR to son from the kitchen (this was before cell phones were in everyone's pockets). That is when we arrived.

I immediately checked for a pulse. Not finding one, I started chest compressions as the senior firefighter, who I will refer to as Jill, on my watch entered the room and began managing respiration. We immediately encountered an issue with opening the airway, so we had a third member enter this small space and support the neck to allow for the airway to open. Keep in mind that time meant nothing to me then, and it did not register in my long-term memory, so it won't be mentioned here as a factor. At some point, I was tapped on the shoulder and looked up at a pair of AED pads. I took them and after cleaning the chest, I attached the pads. I turned around to get the AED, but someone was already holding it out for me. I cleared the casualty, which was not so easy due to the size of the room and the size of us firefighters. When the AED completed its analysis, it came back as "no shock advised". Having taught first aid, I knew exactly what that meant, and continued CPR. I found out we did CPR for approximately 20 minutes while awaiting EMS.

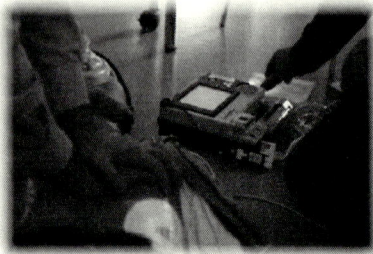

Upon arrival of EMS, the paramedic ordered that the casualty be removed from the bathroom. The members cleared out and the paramedic took the casualty at the arms, and I took the legs. As the paramedic lifted the man's arms and the abdomen folded, the casualty regurgitated onto my shirt. We moved him out onto the floor of the bedroom and I found myself on the neck support role. The new compressor was a newer member and had not done CPR outside of training. He looked unsure and kept asking if he was doing it right. I was able to coach him, andI told him he was doing fine. Finally, the paramedic directed

CPR to stop and it was done. I helped cover the body and pick up the garbage from the floor. It was then that I heard the wail come from the kitchen, such a heartbreaking sound. I think I started to feel claustrophobic, as I remember looking around and thinking there were too many people in this room. Police, paramedics, firefighters, etc.

So, I decided to leave the house and return to my unit. I found the new member sitting alone, so we chatted a bit about the event until another member arrived and pointed out that the son of the casualty was sitting on the front step all alone. I took two bottles of water and sat next to him. As we drank water, he behaved in the expected manner: he didn't do enough to save his dad, he failed, etc. I did my best to assure him that if we couldn't revive him, certainly nothing he had done or not done could have affected the outcome. I put my arm around him and let him cry (if you know me, you would know how much it takes to prompt me into physical contact, like hugs). I stayed with the boy, and eventually a police officer took me aside and asked if I would stay with him as she was putting the family on suicide watch, as I believe the mom had made some concerning comments. Staying with the boy was my intention, so we continued to talk until a friend arrived with his own mom, and I stepped aside.

At around this time, we cleared the scene and returned to the hall. When we were released, we were informed that there would be a debrief scheduled, and I fully intended to participate. I returned home, and immediately shed my shirt and headed for the shower. My wife would never go back to sleep when I was on a call, and she was still awake upon my return. As usual, she asked me what happened. All other calls, I would tell her all about it, but for the very first time, I found that I could not. When she asked, and I opened my mouth to respond, I found myself starting to choke up. So, I told her I would later, and stepped into the shower. When I finished, I lay down and was almost asleep when my phone rang. It was Jill, asking me to return to the scene. When I asked why, she said she did not want to say anything over the phone, and just said she needed me to come back. So, I got dressed again and drove over. I discovered that they required my assistance to load the body into the coroner's van, as he was too heavy for those available. I had to carry the stretcher with the body past the kitchen where some family remained and was once again assaulted by the grief of the family. And then I went home again.

The debrief was held a few days later and was a very eye-opening experience. It was mostly me and Jill who did the talking. Keep in mind, this is the first actual critical incident stress debriefing I had ever had. I remember commenting on how the whole time during the initial work in the bathroom seemed like a well choreographed ballet. I never had to ask for anything. During CPR, everything went like clockwork. I counted off my compressions out loud, and when it came time for respirations and I said "Breathe", Jill squeezed the bag.

When I got to the point when I needed the towel and razor to prepare the chest for the AED, it was there being handed to me. When I completed preparing the chest, the pads were being held out to me. What struck me was Jill's feedback. What I did not know until then was that Jill lived right across the street from the scene and was the friend of our casualty. And I never once got an inkling that Jill was personally involved with this person. She was the ultimate in professionalism at that scene. She also admitted that she was quite upset by it and while I was counting out my compressions, she was adding up the numbers for some odd reason. She also commented that she had looked out the window when I was sitting with my arm around the boy and commented on how much she appreciated the act of kindness. Following this debrief, once again, I had some trouble with just moving on, as I had to drive by the scene everyday on the way out of town. This is just another example of how difficult it is for first responders to work operationally in their own communities. For the first and only time, I attended the funeral of one of my casualties. I was hoping for closure. I do not think I got any, and it was just another trauma stacked up on the rest.

My fourth most memorable call was a single vehicle fire on a remote highway in the winter. The tones went off late in the night. The call details were vague, but someone had reported a fire near the road. Upon arrival, we

discovered a vehicle virtually completely burned. Behind the wheel, we found the driver. The remaining fire was able to be put out by a small fire extinguisher. The floor was littered with what turned out to be bone fragments. The driver's arms, mid humerus, and his legs, mid femur, had fragmented and fell apart. All that remained was the charred torso and head. I had never seen anything like it and seemed sickly drawn toward looking at it. The police arrived, and it was determined that the driver was likely impaired and had driven across a frozen farmer's field, hit the ditch, reversed and accelerated rapidly to overcome the ditch. In doing so, it appears that the propane line in the truck was severed and fuelled the fire. And again, oddly enough, no adverse reaction and another trauma up on the stack.

My fifth, and final, most memorable call was during my last true call prior to leaving the fire department. It was summer, and our town was having its long weekend celebration with tons of activities on the streets. I was happy because I had the weekend off, which was not usual for me. I had planned to spend the day with the family and have some fun. Of course, the tones went off. Bicycle versus car on the highway. Trying to get out of town was difficult as not only were people everywhere, but some of the streets were blocked off. Upon arrival, I saw a car in the opposite ditch with a crowd around it. When I got closer, I saw a person on the trunk of the vehicle. It was apparent that he was very seriously injured. A bystander, who happened to be a paramedic, was tending to him. This was the first time I had interacted with a casualty who was on the verge of death. I remember assisting with log-rolling him onto a backboard when EMS arrived, and I saw his back had been significantly lacerated, so much so that tissue was extruding from the wound. I could hear his laboured breathing and could not help but think he was going to pass away right then. As it turns out, I believe he did pass away *en route* to the hospital.

The cyclist, from across the country, was participating in a group cross-county bike tour. We passed his group while we were responding to the scene. There was some question as to how the collision occurred, but it was left in the hands of the police. It was that summer which was my last on the fire department. I relocated for work, but my family remained behind for a year. When it was time to move the family, I returned home, and it was during the town's long weekend celebration yet again! I decided to swing by the fire hall and say hi and bye. There were a few members standing around chatting, and as I got closer, I realized they were talking about the cyclist from the year before. Someone said that there was someone else at that scene but couldn't remember who it was. As they were not aware I was behind them, I spoke up that it was me, surprising them all! I found out then that the group came back out this way and had contacted the fire department to invite the responders who were involved in the incident to attend a short memorial at the location of the incident. I had just enough time to run home and change into my uniform. It was such a beautiful memorial. The cyclists lined up and proceeded to shake our hands, thank us for what we did, and they had all brought small stones from home and lay them out on the spot. I was so happy to have had the opportunity to participate, and what a wonderful note to end my time on the fire service.

Skip forward a few years of what just seems to be regular life. I had taken a break from the first responder world to teach a protective services program at a college for a couple of years. Following that, I re- entered the field again and managed security at another college. However, I had finally worked hard enough, and the planets aligned for me, and I was able to achieve my law enforcement officer status. It was with a small municipality that contracted patrol services to another nearby town. At first, it was all I could do to not just volunteer before and after my shifts. I loved the job, loved my boss (well, not really, but she was awesome) and very much enjoyed working at the community level.

Shortly after my full credentials were in place, I overheard a page out for the fire department and EMS to attend a possible fatality… and they mentioned my town, and my office was less than twenty seconds from the scene. I attended the scene, once again, first one there, and encountered a hefty set man of approximately late fifties age, crying and frantically telling me that "Something's wrong with my dad". I entered the house and found an elderly male sitting upright on the sofa, with a medium sized dried blood trickle on his face, his face was pale, and he was not moving. As I approached him, I was sure that he was deceased. Sure enough, when I reached out to assess a pulse, it was obvious that he had died days prior. Thankfully, EMS arrived at that time and engaged the man's son. As I left the house, I met the arriving police officer, briefed her and then left the scene. I don't recall feeling anything adverse then either. Just another trauma thrown on the stack.

In the pursuit of my law enforcement duties, I regularly attended medical scenes to provide support until EMS arrived, and attended traffic collisions for the same reason and to support police by assisting with traffic control. During that time, I attended serious collisions and a few fatalities, but never really provided up close and personal intervention, other than the odd first aid. It was not until I was called in to assist a remote community that succumbed to a wildfire that I would, once again, be significantly touched by an experience as a first responder.

A large wildfire burned through the area, which had originated as a forest fire, and quickly spread through fire breaks, and rapidly burned toward the town. The fire forced the complete evacuation of area residents, numbering at approximately seven thousand, and is considered the largest such displacement in the area's history at the time. Amazingly enough, no casualties were reported amongst the town's population. Unfortunately, one first responder was killed in a helicopter mishap while battling the fire. The fire destroyed approximately one-third of the town, and ravaged the surrounding rural areas.

My partner at the time was the one who received the call for help from the town's enforcement officer, and had managed to arrange authorization for us to respond for assistance. This involved a drive of three hours, or so when not driving a police car. I had twenty minutes to pack my gear and be ready to be picked up. I said goodbye to my family and off we went. The entire drive we were passing the mass exodus going south, escaping the flames. We finally encountered a convoy of other emergency response units and fell in behind. As we approached the town at dusk, the horizon looked like you would expect to see in an apocalyptic war movie: the highway was framed by fire ravaged trees, the small brush was still burning along with what grass remained, the road surface was covered in fire retardant powder, and the horizon was ablaze with a throbbing orange light. It was frightening, and I have never seen anything like it before or since. I recall beginning to lose signal on my cell phone, so I called home, told my family I loved them, and then into the fire we drove. Upon arrival into town, we discovered that the town itself was still burning.

When we were able to locate the emergency operations centre, I recall walking into the room, and marvelling at the sheer number of people milling around, checking in, waiting for assignments, etc. I looked over and saw several police officers sitting on the floor and leaning up against the wall. It did not dawn on me at the time as to why, but I remember thinking that they looked shell-shocked. Well, d-uh. I just thought they were tired; they had very rapidly and stressfully faced the fire's approach and evacuated the town. It never even occurred to me that they had also evacuated their own families, and likely knew that their homes burned, and that they lost all. We checked in and were seconded out. I will note that the centre was not expecting us, and had no arrangements made for our accommodations. Thankfully, the police brass took us under their wings, and arranged rooms for us. I was assigned to a rural evacuation team. We were ensuring areas were evacuated and removing those who had previously been evacuated and who had returned.

At the time, I found the experience exhilarating. I was amazed at the utter mystery of the fire and it's burning pattern. At one house, as I was banging on the front door, and moving on to check the perimeter, I heard my teammate call for me. She pointed out the that the unattached garage was burned to the ground. The odd thing was that the house was only a few metres away and yet the siding on the house was not ever remotely warped from the heat. We would see fence lines burned completely, but a single fence panel in the middle completely untouched, vehicles parked side by side and only one burned, and how the flames would entirely skip a property, leaving the grass un-singed, but the next property utterly destroyed. If you're a firefighter, you'll know what I'm talking about. One vivid memory is coming upon a burning building, and seeing people running in and out throwing materials out of the building. I remember the officer I was with saying "What the fuck is this?!" and when we got closer, we realized it was a rural fire hall that was on fire, and that the people were the firefighters trying to save their equipment, necessary for the emergency. Again, it never struck me how this would impact those firefighters in the aftermath.

At the end of that initial 12-hour shift, I was assigned a hotel room, as there was literally nowhere else to go, and I was completely exhausted. Unfortunately for me, I was on the fourth floor. The town's electrical system was out, but there was electricity at the hotel provided by generators, but no water except small individual drinking bottles. In order to wash, and it was completely necessary due to being coated in ash and other assorted toxic junk, I had to resort to sponge bathing out of the toilet tank with cold water, no showers. The lack of hot water really wasn't that much of a hardship, as we were directed to refrain from washing or shaving with hot water,

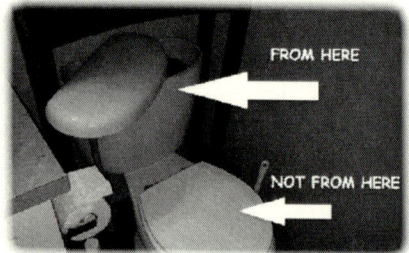

as they were concerned about anything that would open our pores and be exposed to the toxic chemicals in the air. I would bail some water from the toilet tank into the sink and hope that that water left in the tank would last me. Otherwise, I'd be humping water back to my hotel room. Remember, I could not use the toilet, as I would lose my water supply. I will spare you the gory details about what I used for a toilet.

If you have ever worked an emergency such as this, you will know how very important food is to maintain your energy, both physical and mental. Due to being there during the initial stages of the disaster, food was in short supply. It mostly consisted of dry goods that didn't need refrigeration. I think I lived on granola bars and juice boxes. We were fortunate enough that the owner of the local grocery store, facing the expiration of the food in the store due to the lack of electricity, brought what food was available. We ate better then, but that depleted quickly.

The next two twelve-hour shifts were patrolling the town and assisting with road blocks. The first day of town patrol was devastating to me, seeing entire neighbourhoods utterly destroyed, water still spraying from the pipes in the foundations, natural gas pipes with the gas still burning, burned vehicles with nothing left but the metal. I took several photos of the destruction I saw. But the photos do no justice. Some of the buildings were still hot, and flames intermittently licked up. There is one photo that stands out amongst all the others. It is of the yard of a burned home. The yard is just soot, and there

appears to be what once was a patio set: chairs and a table, nothing but bare metal frames now. In the middle of the soot, away from everything else, sits a blue plastic table, melted. There is also a pink child-sized papa-san chair, looking untouched by the fire. However, right next to the melted table is the burned frame of another papa-san chair, but it's just the metal frame. This broke my heart and brought all the pain associated with this sheer devastation home, and no longer was I able to look at my environment and just think in terms of a first responder or strictly as a homeowner. I now saw things from the perspective of a father, and my heart ached for all the children who lost everything they owned and cherished. Thankfully, kids are significantly more resilient than us old folk. I was also rocked by the sheer devastation I was seeing. Entire neighbourhoods destroyed, homes burned right down into the foundations, nothing left except the pipes, husks of appliances and furnaces, and the springs and frames from box springs and mattresses. It was this last photo that I feel broke the dam finally and brought my issues to the forefront of my life.

For the remainder of the time I spent there, I assisted with pet rescue operations. A social media site had been created by some volunteers, and in conjunction with the local enforcement officer, I participated in a round-up of pets who had bolted during the frenzied evacuation or those who were left in their homes. We had been given permission to break into homes to remove the pets, and a temporary shelter was formed for the animals. Thankfully, all the pets I had rescued were all in good health, so I guess that spared me some trauma, as I am an animal guy.

When I was released and went home, I was fatigued (having just worked 12 hours and no sleep, no debrief, no nothing, just a quick thank you and off we went. I was sitting in the passenger seat, and since I was not driving, all I had to do was sit and think. I was physically and emotionally exhausted, but I felt a bubble in me that was growing. All the stress of the past few days finally had a chance to try to escape. Although I was not sure what it was, I was sure that I didn't want it to burst while I was in the patrol car with my partner. All I can say about that was that it was a long ride home.

CHAPTER 3

The Story of IAN

This is the story of Ian, a correctional peace officer for thirteen years, that was until he had to retire. He was thirty-three years old at the time of his retirement. He really enjoyed his employment as a correctional officer for the first couple of years. He was proud to tell people what he did for a living, and he was proud to be a member of the law enforcement community. Then things in his life changed.

In 2006, Ian was involved in a motor vehicle collision on his way home from work for lunch. It was not a serious collision, but still bad enough that it took him out of commission for a significant period of time. He could not move his left arm properly for about a month or so, and since he could not perform regular duties, he could not attend work. During this time, he started to suffer from depression and anxiety. He did not connect this to his work in any way. He had been a correctional peace officer for five years at this time. He reached out and asked for help from the local mental health authority to deal with the anxiety and depression, but was told that there was a wait, and he was placed on a waiting list.

In 2007, Ian attempted suicide by slitting his own throat. He does not remember much of what actually happened, and he believes that his mind has blocked some of it out as a defense. What he does remember from that day is that he walked out of his place of employment late that night and walked to his car. He remembers getting into his car and remembers turning into his condo complex. However, he does not remember the drive itself. After that, he remembers waking up on his kitchen floor with a knife in his hand and blood on his neck where he had cut. He knows that he was lucky that he did not cut deep enough to cause severe injury. Following this suicide attempt, he decided to demand help from his local mental health authority, as he still had not been seen by anyone.

Ian started seeing a counsellor locally, and it was helping a bit, but she could only do so much. They would meet every two weeks to talk and work on his mental health. Approximately three months into his therapy, his counsellor suggested he may benefit from some medical intervention as well and asked if he was open to seeing a psychiatrist. Ian agreed, and started seeing a doctor with his counsellor at the meetings, as well. He was wrongfully diagnosed at that time with Bi-Polar Disorder Type 2 and would be treated as such for the next three or four years. He accepted this diagnosis, and faithfully used the medication he was prescribed. However, the medication had little to no effect on his symptoms but came with a host of side effects. He still to this date suffers from some of them.

Ian lived his life for a considerable time as someone who thought he had bipolar disorder. He had been off work while the medication the psychiatrist prescribed regulated themselves in his system. After several months, he was able to return to work. He returned to work on full duties at the correctional centre and was happy to do so. Unfortunately, his feelings changed once he realized how people were acting around him.

Working in law enforcement, and especially in a confined place like a correctional centre, it is necessary to be able to trust partners - to protect and assist. When Ian returned to work, he was ready to go to back up any officer that needed his help without a second thought. The problem was, some of the officers found out about his diagnosis, and decided they did not want to have Ian back them up or even be on the same unit with him. He did not notice anything different for roughly his first two months back, but then he began to understand the dynamics of his issues with work. He was not being assigned to work with the same staff for more than two days in a row. They would put newly hired staff with him, but never senior staff. People would move away when he was in the lunch room and would not talk to him. Ian felt he was being ostracized because people did not understand. Some people would talk to him and want to know what bipolar disorder was all about, so he would try to explain it, but felt like it fell on deaf ears. People had too many preconceptions of what having mental health issues meant. In Ian's opinion, he felt his coworkers did not want to be around someone like him, because they were afraid of him.

After a while of being ostracized, Ian decided to request a transfer to the mental health unit. His request was granted, and he was placed as the acting case worker on that unit. He worked that position for two and a half years with primarily the same partner. When Ian's partner transferred to another centre, Ian stayed on the unit for about six months, and then he ended up going on to a rotation of night shifts. Before his night shifts were done, Ian asked his manager if he would let him manage the segregation unit, as that way he would be away from the offenders and not have to worry about other officers acting odd around him. Ian would be working alone inside a little fish tank of a work station. Once again, his request was granted, and he remained running this unit for the last two and a half years of his career.

During his time working on his facility's mental health unit. In addition to working with the offenders on the unit, Ian was also in charge of case work for a program that was specific to sexual offenders at an off-site location. He was required to read their files, and know what their charges were, and what the circumstances of those cases. He would have to talk to the offenders about the crimes and discuss matters with offenders' families. He would also have to complete release planning for offenders and complete any police notification letters for when offenders were being released. Ian is the father of three small children, with his oldest being a girl and most of the charges he had to review involved young female victims the same age. That position was not easy on his mental health!

When Ian had decided he was unable to continue in the mental health unit, he moved to the segregation unit. He was working alone. He was away from the offenders and away from everyone else. At that time, he felt that was right for him, and he believes it actually hindered him. The offenders that he dealt with in segregation were the ones that could not live with the rest of the offender population. They were in segregation for their own safety, for disciplinary reasons, or because if they had to live on a regular unit they would kill someone. He was charged with keeping them safe from themselves, as well as from the other offenders.

While operating the segregation unit, he was relatively healthy. His mind was in a good spot, the medications seemed to be working properly, and his anxiety and other symptoms seemed to be getting under control. Apparently, he was wrong! Nearing the end of 2013, the facility's management decided to move staff around. One day, his direct supervisor came to his unit about halfway through his shift to inform Ian that they were moving him from segregation, a maximum-security unit, to a common residential unit. This was a fully open concept unit, where the offenders are in open bunk beds and no cells at all - they were out in the open with full privileges. Ian was to start working on the dorms at the beginning of his next rotation.

Ian's first day on the dorms unit would also be his last day of being on a unit in the correctional centre. He walked on to the unit very anxious and worried. He started to calm down a bit part way through his shift, but that did not last long at all. He was conducting a patrol of the unit, when one of the offenders addressed him, and said nine simple words that he will never forget, and they have haunted him ever since the offender uttered them.

"They let you out of the hole, hey Boss?"

That is all he said. He didn't threaten Ian, he didn't yell at him, nothing. He just said those nine little words, and that triggered Ian. He still does not understand why, but those nine little words ended his career in corrections. He could not move once he completed his rounds. He sat behind his desk and could do nothing. He reported that he was, for lack of a better term, "scared stiff".

For the next two days, Ian was at meetings at the union hall. He was a very active member of the correctional services' union and was the union's co-chair of the human rights committee at the time. He went to the meetings for two days with the union, and afterward, it was determined that he was to return for the rest of his shifts. He woke up the morning of what should have been his next shift, but was so frozen with anxiety, he could not move out of bed. He called in sick that day, and never returned to regular duties. He was off work for the majority of 2014.

Ian went from doctor to doctor, trying to figure out what was wrong with him, why he was suddenly so anxious about going to work at a job that he had loved for so long. He finally returned to the psychiatrist that originally diagnosed him with bipolar disorder. The psychiatrist re-evaluated everything that Ian was telling him, and he realized that Ian had been misdiagnosed. Ian started seeing a counsellor again and was encouraged to apply to the local workers compensation board, as he was suffering from a work-related injury.

Ian was evaluated against the post-traumatic stress disorder. The assessment resulted in the determination that Ian did not have one or two specific incidents that triggered his disorder, rather it was the combination of years of traumatic stress from working in such a negative environment. He was further informed that he had to meet all five of the specific criteria to be able to qualify, and if he did not meet all five, he would be denied. Ian met four of the five with no doubt, but because the job he worked for thirteen years was not above what another correctional peace officer would have to do, he was denied coverage.

Regardless, Ian did not do any work that was above what another correctional peace officer would have to do, but it had affected him greatly. He attempted to file a compensation claim and was told that, because he was a correctional peace officer, he would not qualify for presumptive coverage, as he was not *"technically"* considered a first responder. He was told time and time again that, due to his classification not qualifying him for presumptive coverage, he was made to prove that his post-traumatic stress disorder was the result of specific incidents at work, and not just an accumulation over the years. This made him feel like he was not supported at all, and completely invalidated the effort he was making to improve his mental health.

Ian continued worked with his long-term disability liaison worker, because no matter what he did, the compensation board would not accept his claim. His worker had Ian sent to a new counsellor that specialized in post-traumatic stress disorder for first responders, who evaluated Ian once again. The counsellor told Ian at the end of the very first visit that he believed that Ian was suffering from classic cumulative post-traumatic stress disorder. Ian attended counselling for four months, and the help he gave Ian was the best he had receive to date. Unfortunately, Ian hit another road block, as his long-term disability policy would not cover any further sessions. He could not afford to pay the cost of the sessions out of pocket, so he had to end his therapy.

From the time Ian went off work, until the day he submitted his letter of resignation at the end of 2014, he felt he was treated as someone that just wanted to milk the system. When he initially met with the disability coordinator that was to set up his "*return to work*" program, he was told one thing about the program, but it ended up being something completely different. He was told that he would not be going back to full duties, and that his return to work would be gradual. However, the form Ian was given to sign at his meeting with management indicated "*full duties*" immediately from the first day back. He met with the employer and the disability coordinator to discuss the return to work, and he was told he was to return to his position within days. He contacted the employer and his disability representative to further discuss the matter, as he was feeling very uncomfortable with the idea of such a quick transition back after so many months off. He was told that the disability company would not set up a new meeting, and that he was to report to work on the date indicated. He informed them that he felt he was not ready, and was told that if he did not return on the planned date, he would be immediately removed from disability benefits and the department would have full control of his future from there. Ian understood this to mean that if he did not return on the assigned date, he would be removed from sick leave, and if he did not return, he could, and most likely would be fired for not returning as ordered. This would also mean that if terminated, Ian would forfeit thirteen years of employer-paid pension benefits.

With a wife and three small children at home to support, being fired just was not an option. He went home and discussed his predicament with his wife and explained how worried he was about what felt like a forced return to work. They figured that he basically had three options at this time:

1. Return to work against his better judgement on the assigned date and risk having a major incident happen, in which he could get hurt, someone else could be hurt or worse;

2. Not return to work on the assigned date and risk being terminated, or;

3. Resign his position and attempt to move on with his life.

They decided on the third option as it felt like the only viable one they had at the time. Ian felt like he was being forced out of the service. A few days before the assigned return date, he walked into the correctional centre and handed in his resignation, effective immediately. In his letter, he explained in no uncertain terms, exactly how he felt about the whole situation. To Ian's surprise, his manager on duty tried to refuse his resignation. They contacted the union and asked them if they could convince Ian to reconsider, or even to just re-write his resignation letter. The union called Ian and asked what he wanted them to do. Ian told the union to call his employer back and laugh at them. Ian believed that the facility's management wanted him to return to work so they could fire him and have the upper hand. Ian was not going to allow them to do that to him and his family, after the way they treated him.

Once Ian retired, he was still off work for a couple months due to a death in the family, as well as the challenging task of finding an employer that would hire him after so many years of nothing but security and law enforcement related experience. Months later, he started his first new job in fourteen years! He started at a local radio station, as an advertising salesman. The pay was not great, but it kept his family fed until he could find something better. Still months later, he started as a salesman at a local auto dealership, where he remains. He loves his new career, and he has never been happier in a work environment that he currently works, and truly believes that taking this job is one of the best things he has ever done. He believes that he still owes the owner of the dealership a major debt of gratitude, for taking a chance on someone that is suffering from post-traumatic stress disorder and allowing him the opportunity to show them what he can achieve. By giving Ian his second chance, his new employer is helping to break the stigma of mental health issues. They have helped Ian to continue up his "*stairway to closure*" and make a new life for himself and his family.

However, the result of the trauma experienced throughout his thirteen years of correctional service, Ian will battle this illness for the rest of his life. He still has dreams and nightmares of incidents that occurred during his time in corrections. Ian suffers from blackouts, panic attacks, and while he is working hard to identify triggers, he cannot always prevent it. Some days are good, and some are horrible.

CHAPTER 4

The Story of JOHN

John is a thirty-five-year-old paramedic and has worked in EMS for over thirteen years in rural and urban settings. He was an Emergency Medical Technician for ten years and has been a paramedic for the last three years. John has also worked as an auxiliary law enforcement officer since 2005 and still holds his peace officer status.

John has enjoyed his work for the most part and found it to be very satisfying. Things began to change however in 2009. He responded to a call in a small rural municipality for a four-year-old girl who had been crushed by an elevator in a home. She was playing half inside and half outside of it when someone on another floor called the elevator. It operated on a pulley system so there were no safety mechanisms in place. The elevator came down and crushed her trachea. They called for the local air ambulance to transport her to the nearest children's hospital. Upon arrival at the hospital, they took her to surgery where she bled out and died on the operating room table. John had attended many terrible calls up until this point but for some reason, he could not let this one go. He pushed it to the back of his head and tried to move on.

A couple months later John responded to a call on the highway at that very same small municipality for a motor vehicle collision. John could tell immediately that this one was not going to be like the many collisions he had attended before. There were two cars involved. As they rolled up, John could see one person laying on the ground, some bystanders on the side of the road, and an off-duty firefighter and a police officer on scene. When they stopped, his partner was exiting the passenger side of the ambulance when a woman approached her holding a six-month-old baby who was silent and covered in blood. She handed his partner the baby and began crying. His partner looked at him and he told her to go into the ambulance and take care of the child while he checked on everyone else. John sent a firefighter into the ambulance to help his partner just as a police officer told him the woman in the car closest to them was still alive.

John grabbed his bags and went down. There was so much damage to the car that John had to reach in through the sunroof to check for a pulse. John was unable to feel one. John looked in the backseat and could see a car seat. This was the baby's mother. Due to the fact John had to triage more people, he was unable to dedicate any time to trying to help this patient. As John pulled his arms out from the sunroof, he saw that he had brain matter stuck to his skin. He did not think anything of it and just brushed it off. He looked at the woman again but couldn't see any head trauma. Where did this come from?

John went over to the woman laying on the ground. It had become quickly apparent she was the source of the brain matter. Her injuries were incompatible with life, so he moved on. There were two more women in the next car. He could see they both had critical injuries, and upon a quick exam he determined they were both deceased. He now turned his attention to the baby in the ambulance. He opened the door and saw the firefighter standing there, pale, wanting out. He told him to get out of the ambulance. Another ambulance arrived, and they took one of their crew members in the back of the ambulance. STARS air ambulance was going to meet them at the nearest hospital, so he started driving. When they arrived, they took the baby into the emergency department where they handed over care to the ER staff and the STARS crew. He and his partner stood back and watched. John personally felt drained but what he had seen hadn't hit him yet. When the helicopter left without the patient, John looked at his partner and she asked if he was ok. He lied and said yes. When he asked if she was ok she lied and said yes, however her bottom lip quivered a little and John had to leave. John went out to the ambulance, sat in the driver seat, and suddenly, he began to cry. He did not know why, and it was unlike anytime he had cried before. He had been to dozens of terrible calls. Why was this one any different? John continued to let it all out, not even sure what he was letting out. Then he heard someone coming out. It was another paramedic. John tried to compose himself, but she could tell there was an issue. She sent someone to get his supervisor. You must remember, while this wasn't that long ago, there was still a severe stigma that if you had a breakdown on a call, you weren't fit for the job. John didn't want to get a reputation for being a terrible practitioner. He didn't want people talking about him, and making jokes.

His supervisor came out. He asked if John was ok. Immediately he started to cry. His supervisor grabbed John by his jacket, pulled him out of the ambulance and gave him a big hug. According to John, this supervisor is one of the pioneers of EMS, and just the kindest man you've ever met. As he hugged him, John just couldn't control it and began to soak the shoulder of his supervisor's jacket.

Just as a side note, John was writing all of this on his laptop in a pub, and as he was writing his story down, he had tears in his eyes. This is a call that will be with him forever and elicits an emotional response every time he talks about it. After a couple of minutes John was able to somewhat compose himself. The executive director of his ambulance service came in on his day off, took them for coffee and offered them all the support they needed.

Over the next four days, John was in close contact multiple times daily with his partner as both were struggling. John was constantly Googling the accident, collecting articles from the paper and just generally becoming obsessed. A few days later, he attended a memorial service for three of the girls who were in the one car. He hoped it would bring him some closure. There was a large balloon release. Afterwards, John saw the parents. He wanted to go up to them and apologize to them. Apologize for his shortcoming in not being able to help their children. Apologize that he was unable to do the one thing he was supposed to do: which is help people. John was carrying around so much guilt from this call, knowing that there was nothing he could do. In the end he left without saying anything. As he was driving home, he began to have another breakdown. He had to pull over on the side of the road as he could not see through the tears. John contacted his employee assistance program to seek out help. He would not get into the details of the program as he found absolutely no help from it what so ever. The therapist to which he was assign stated she was unable to help him and had nobody she could refer him to so John just pushed his emotions back further and tried to just shut off the bad feelings.

John was contacted by the parents and aunt of one of the girls killed in the crash. They asked if he could meet them for coffee, and he agreed. In his mind, while he was struggling with the events that had occurred, it was nothing compared to what they were going through. He met them at their house. They asked him questions about who was driving, and what he had seen. John was very vague with what he had seen because he didn't want them to get a picture in their minds of what he had seen. He wanted them to remember their daughter as a vibrant young woman who was enjoying her life. They mentioned that they were finding ways to move forward and try to cope. They thanked him for his time and they parted ways. John hoped that he was able to give them closure. All the girls were between the ages of seventeen and nineteen.

The following year, a colleague of his from when he worked in northern rural area on an ambulance service was killed when his ambulance collided with a propane tank that separated from a semi truck tractor. The police collision analysts stated they concluded he steered the ambulance to take the hit head on because it was originally going to hit the rear compartment where his partner was attending to a child. The child's mother was also in the back. When they collided, the ambulance rolled into the ditch, and when it came to a stop, the surviving paramedic, unaware of any injuries she had sustained, put the little girl and her mom in a passerby's truck and told them to drive to the hospital. She went around to the driver side of the ambulance and found her partner in agonal respirations. Agonal respirations are when your brain is making a last-ditch effort to stay alive by trying to facilitate breathing, but all your other body systems have shut down. It does not count as actual breathing. She attempted to perform CPR on him, not realizing she herself had a broken arm and a lung that had collapsed. She was taken by air ambulance to the hospital and her partner was pronounced dead at the scene. John went up for his memorial service with a few former colleagues. They had to go into the basement of the church and watch on a projector screen as there were so many people that not everyone could fit. First responders from all over North America came out to show their respects. They brought his casket into the church draped with a flag. He does not remember much from the service, but he does remember hearing the different way he helped people and changed their lives from working as a teacher until his retirement, then continuing to work as a substitute teacher and working on the ambulance. He was always helping people, and did so up until his last breaths. It made John unbelievably proud to know and work with him. At the same time, he felt a great loss. According the John, this man was a hero. Not by his own admission, but by the way lived. He was the embodiment of why John got into the job. And now he was dead.

Fast forward 3 years. John was still working on the ambulance but in a new station and with a new partner. Life seemed to be going well. He was working a ton of overtime, buying lots of cool toys. One day, John hears a story on the radio about how some thieves were breaking into vehicles and stealing contents. It had said they had stolen a box and poured out the contents which ended up being someone's ashes. While being terrible, it did not really affect him. When he got home that night, he opened the newspaper and immediately he had seen a picture of one of the girls from the fatal collision he had been to a few years back.

Her mother had been carrying her daughter's ashes around with her this entire time. The thieves had poured the ashes into the gutter during a rain storm and they washed down the storm drain. This was a turning point for him. He does not know what happened, he just felt nothing. If you have never experienced the feeling of feeling absolutely nothing, it is truly a terribleplace to be. It was in this moment John realized why people self-harm when they are suffering from depression: such as cut their skin, or take pills. These things make you feel something; while it might be something unpleasant, the feeling of pain is better than the feeling of nothing or emptiness. John took a sleeping pill to make himself go to sleep, and went to work the next day. He still felt an endless emptiness, but he put on a smiling face, so nobody would notice.

He finished his shift, went home and back into emptiness. Scenes from the crash kept coming back into his mind. Flashbacks that he couldn't stop. A cycle of pain and death kept filling his mind, but it still didn't make him feel anything. He needed this to stop; he needed out of this. Reaching out and making a phone call was not an option for him for some reason. He could not ask for help because the last time he did, he felt that he was let down. He asked himself what else could he do to help himself?

He went into his bedroom and grabbed his .40 calibre Smith and Wesson handgun. John loaded a round into it, and sat on the floor. He told me that the only solution for him was to put the gun to his head, pull the trigger and end things. That was the only way he felt he could think of to stop the visuals. Just then, he felt sick to his stomach. Now the images change to something that made him feel something. All he could imagine was someone having to call his mom and tell her that he was found dead in his basement from a self-inflicted gunshot wound to the head.

Imagining her having to have his brains cleaned up from the walls; having to make the arrangements to bury her only child. The pain that he knew he would have caused her was the only thing that stopped him from killing himself that night. John went to work the next day, and he had a closed door talk with his supervisor. He laid everything out. From the initial calls, to siting in his basement one thought away from killing himself. John has difficulty expressing enough how liberating it felt to get everything out in the open to someone, and to have that person do everything in their power to help him. He told me that he can say with all honesty that his supervisor saved his life.

John was placed into a PTSD rehabilitation program with the local workers compensation authority. He worked with three psychologists, and an occupational therapist daily for months. It was a valuable experience for him and helped him to move passed many of the issues he was having. One thing he wanted to make clear is that he had no desire to die. He just didn't want to live. It might seem difficult to grasp the concept. As much as he did not want to die, he did not want to live in the emptiness that he had felt anymore.

John returned to work after two months of being in his rehabilitation program. He could feel things again. He still had thoughts of death, but he still didn't want to die, and he now had some tools to help deal with things going on in his head. Now he started to see mental health issues as being no different from physical health issues, because they are not any different. They are both equally important to our well being and need to be addressed by professionals.

Things had been going well for a couple years. John was now a new paramedic in 2014, working with another new partner. They got a call for a gunshot wound one night in another small rural municipality. The standard procedure is that when there is a firearm on scene, EMS is to stage a few blocks away and wait for the police to secure the scene. Unfortunately, his partner made a mistake navigating and they were staged right out front of the patient's house. A woman was waving her arms at them. They couldn't just drive away so he told his partner he would go in first as he had a bullet proof vest on. He went inside and, in a bedroom, found a sixteen-year-old male with a self-inflicted shotgun wound to the head. Inside his room there was brain and skull all over the roof and walls. He was sitting cross legged with shotgun resting up against his neck. He was obviously deceased. The woman waving at them was the victim's mother and she was understandably hysterical. She began to scream "I can't find [her other child]! Where is [her other child]!" They began to search the house, looking for another potential body. They searched inside, around the outside of the house and down the street. He was finally located at a friend's house and had not seen what happened to his brother. They stayed on scene and waited for the police. They spoke to the mother to get information they needed and to try to console her. Her family arrived including the father and grandfather of the deceased.

When the police arrived, John and his partner cleared from the scene to minimize how many people were there. They went to grab something to eat afterwards but when they got the restaurant, John wasn't hungry. His partner made a joke asking if he was alright because he wasn't hungry for once. He said he was fine but that his stomach was just a bit upset. When they got back to the station, John stayed in the ambulance bay while his partner went inside. He could feel things starting to get spun up in his head. All he could see were imagines of the dead kid while hearing his mother screaming.

He called his supervisor to tell him he needed to take the rest of the shift off. His supervisor asked if he was ok. John told him he had to go, and he hung up the phone. He immediately lay down on the concrete and began hyperventilating and crying again. His partner came out and found him in that state. His partner helped calm him down and they called the supervisor back to update him. John left the station and, on his way home, he began to feel some pain in his chest and was starting to breath rapidly. He stopped at a hospital and was given a prescription for medication which is commonly used to treat anxiety. I quote John, "A paramedic who gets anxiety from doing his job? This isn't going to go well."

This was the beginning of his issues of being afraid of the dark. It wasn't so much the dark he was afraid of. It was the ghosts he would see in them. Anytime he opened his eyes, or walked down a dark hallway at home, he would see the sixteen-year-old who shot himself. He would be standing there as clearly as any real person. John would have to turn all the lights on in the house anytime he got up at night. Even when his eyes were closed, he would feel him standing there, beside his bed looking at him. If he opened his eyes, there his victim was. Staring at him. This hallucination wouldn't leave him alone. Then came the nightmares. One of the worst nightmares was one where the victim's mom was attacking John, screaming at him for not helping her son. When he awoke, he found he was using his hands to block the punches he was experiencing in his dreams. For weeks he experienced these hallucinations, seeing dead people, waking up from nightmares multiple times a night. He knew he needed help and went back into his PTSD rehabilitation program. Again, he spent a couple months getting help. He realized this just might be a new part of his job, where he would have to go in for a "brain tune up" (I love that phrase!) essentially every few years. After completing his program again, he was able to sleep. He is still not a fan of the dark though, but the ghost sighting has decreased tremendously.

John is now a first contact for many people in his workplace who are struggling with mental stress, post traumatic stress disorder and other mental health issues. This is because, admirably, he can be very open about his experiences. He fell though the cracks and the system failed him. He says that he does not want that to happen to anyone else, and that he wants to use his experiences to help others get the help they need. It became apparent to him that even before that first call with the four-year-old and that call with the four girls who were killed, he was suffering. However, he always pretended to be happy because he didn't want to bring others down. What he didn't realize is that he wouldn't have brought his friends down, but they would have helped bring him up. Your friends and coworkers are vital to be a main support structure in your mental stress recovery.

A quote that John thinks perfectly sums up his experience with mental health issues is from the late Robin Williams, who unfortunately lost his battle with mental help demons. Williams said:

"I think the saddest people always try their hardest to make people happy because they know what it's like to feel absolutely worthless and they don't want anyone else to feel like that."

CHAPTER 5

When the Chickens Come Home to Roost

While it may be an odd analogy to make, I feel it's quite apt. It seemed that suddenly, all my symptoms of stress started to occur. Or maybe a better analogy is that of the dominoes, and that the catalyst that started this whole adventure down the path of mental health wonderland was the first domino, and the rest just fell in line. Or perhaps it's the finger in the dam metaphor, where the pressure built up over time finally exceeded the capacity. Who knows. Analogies aside, when it started, it really came on hard.

When I got home from the wildfire, fortunately my children were at school. I sat down on the sofa and started to talk to my wife about the experience. Before long, I was bawling my eyes out in the arms of my wife. After that, and a good night sleep, I thought that would be it. I had always been able to cope with my life stresses, so I didn't expect this to be any different. I suspect that a debrief would not have prevented my chickens coming home to roost, but I do believe it would have helped me process the experience and the underlying emotional trauma that I had suffered unbeknown to me at the time. I got to relive the experience shortly thereafter, when I attended a local fund-raiser for the displaced residents. I had created a PowerPoint presentation of the photos I took and relayed the story of the experience to attendees.

Not long after my return, I began having jaw fatigue and pain. Shortly following the beginning of the fatigue, the muscles seized up in my jaw. I looked like a hamster with the mumps. Not really feeling sick, I was concerned that perhaps I had something wrong with my lymph nodes in my neck, so I went to the hospital and the doctor told me it wasn't nodes or anything like that, and that it was likely just stress. He then recommended that I consult a dentist. I followed his advice, and the dentist found the same; no structural issues. She also

believed that the muscle seizure was likely stress, and she gave me exercises for my jaw. Little did I know, this was the beginning of my body and mind revolt.

Over the next few years, my physical and emotional wellbeing was a roller-coaster. I started suffering headaches (a few of which were migraines), but the headaches lasted for days. I then developed tendinitis in my elbows, which ended up reducing my grip strength significantly and caused serious pain. I was having generalized muscle pains and muscle twitches. My twitches became very disruptive, especially when I was asleep, as they would wake me up and would disturb my wife's ability to sleep as well. Next, I started to experience numbness in my fingers and hands, sometimes in my forearms. These were always pre-migraine indicators but found that they did not always precede migraines. I eventually underwent nerve induction testing, and the doctor found no neural issues.

The one major issue that I hid from everyone was the constant wanting to cry. I knew that if I just had one good cathartic outburst of the emotion inside of me, things would improve. Tragically, at around this time, an incident had occurred that involved the murder of a group of police officers on the other side of the country. Being a law enforcement officer, it hit very close to the heart. I knew I would watch the funeral, and I knew I would be a wreck. I thought that this might be just the opportunity that I was looking for. So, I recorded the funeral, so I could watch it without the kids getting freaked out by dad losing his mind. When the time came, I got my box of Kleenex, settled into the sofa, hit play and… nothing. It did not record for some reason. ROBBED! Not only did I miss the funeral but lost was the opportunity for me to get it out. What I do not know is what it would have done for me in retrospect. All I do know is that I never had another opportunity.

Following this lost opportunity, I started having interesting responses to highly charged emotional situations, but not how you would think. I have responded to numerous tragedies over the course of my career, and that has not changed recently. I am not talking about the classic post-traumatic stress responses you're probably familiar with. My responses haven't caused me night terrors, exaggerated and/or inappropriate emotional outbursts, self-medication, relational breakdown or any such dysfunctional behaviours. I have friends who suffer from diagnoses of post-traumatic stress disorder, one who found it necessary to leave law enforcement career to heal, and a paramedic who was fortunately able to remain in his chosen field, but only after significant therapy. However, I began having disconcerting emotional reactions to certain situations I encountered on TV and online, with content that ranges on the continuum of very sad to very happy. It was then that the Internet was rife with videos of deceased soldiers returning from operational combat zones. These videos, as you know, just show up without warning. More so for me, due to the sites I was following at the time. It was also a time when there were numerous police line-of-duty deaths, and the resulting funeral videos.

I found I was unable to contain myself, and at the least I would find my chin trembling and getting choked up and at the most finding myself crying. As if this was not already difficult to manage, I then found myself reacting the very same way when the media was happy, for example, when returning soldiers were reunited with family, especially when it was a surprise. You will probably remember the plethora of these videos where these soldiers would surprise their families and their children. I could not contain my emotions one way or the other.

And then the next big hit. As I began to revisit the idea of a big cry, a crippling fear grabbed me. I got to the point where I was terrified at the prospect of not being able to stop crying if I started. Can you imagine how utterly horrific it is to face the potential of losing such control over yourself? I was so afraid of that happening, that I struggled even more as my emotions ran away from me whenever I saw these videos, or I saw a news report. I thought that I had developed a hypersensitivity to grief, but by then, it was also the happy situations that made people cry that would trigger me. It was a hypersensitivity to high emotion that was triggering me. Knowing that, however, did nothing to make it better. I struggled with this for a couple more years. And no... I did not seek help... and I still do not know why... well, I do know... I was afraid of what would come of it all.

The next revolt involved my heart. I began to experience heart palpitations. They started intermittently and infrequently, just like I had experienced my whole life (of course, back then I had no idea what they really were). However, they grew in frequency until I was experiencing hundreds every day. It was then that my wife ratted me out to my doctor. I was with her at an appointment for some other matter.

At the end of the appointment, she turns to me and told me to tell him. My doctor, who was a young doctor, a very good doctor, asked what was going on. So, I told him everything. He knew what I did for a living, but initially he was more concerned that I may be suffering from a heart issue. I underwent tests immediately, and they proved that there was nothing structurally wrong with my heart. At the follow up appointment, he disclosed that he had personal experience with depression and anxiety due to the suffering of family members, and he was sure that was what was going on with me. Of course, due to my occupation, he brought up post-traumatic stress disorder. I told him that I did not have PTSD, as I knew a fair bit about it, and that I was lacking some of the criteria. He looked at my wife and said, "See? Denial." I laughed, and told him I was not in denial, it was just the truth. I told him that I am very self-aware, and that I would know if I was that bad off. He then looked at my wife and said, "See? Hypersensitivity." My doctor was that way, a good sense of humour. He insisted that he start a local workers compensation authority claim, and arranged for an assessment for me.

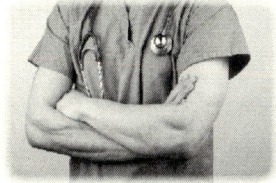

I attended the assessment with a psychologist. I filled out the questionnaires, sat in the interview and talked. I have no concerns over ego to overcome, and so I was candid about my history, my experiences, and my symptoms. I saw a psychologist and was told that I did not meet the criteria for PTSD. So, I went back to my doctor all ready to be smug and self-righteous and say, "I told you so!". Again, he and I had a pretty easy doctor/patient relationship. He, in no uncertain terms, would not believe that, but abided by it. Since the symptoms were the same, I started treatment for depression and anxiety. At this same time, I reached out to my local mental health office to a colleague there, and she put me in front of their psychiatrist for an actual psychiatric evaluation. Following a very ineffective session with a counsellor, I then saw a psychiatrist for a clinical psychiatric evaluation. This resulted in a diagnosis of Generalized Anxiety Disorder and a Major Depressive Disorder. He came back with the same diagnosis and supported the medication I was prescribed. As it turns out, the heart palpitations were panic attacks. He prescribed an antidepressant he had had success with other patients with the same diagnosis.

But it was too late. I very quickly spiralled down into a very serious depressive state. I lost all motivation for anything around me, including my family. It was all I could do to keep up appearances while at work and to be able to maintain my professionalism with my contact with the public. My temper was the worst I have ever know it to be, and I was flying off the handle in situations that were very inappropriate and was very hurtful to my family. By the time I would come home from work, I would walk past everyone and

just lay on the bed, turn on the TV and just be a breathing, heart beating blob of nothing.

I remember one incident when my wife came into the bedroom and looked right at me and asked incredulously if I had not heard my daughter ask me a question? I had no idea what she was talking about, and it seems that I just walked right past my daughter as she was talking to me and walked away. Did not ever register that she was standing right there.

It was during this depressive state, and the medication side-effects that kicked in (of which there were many, lucky me), that created a whole new dimension to my mental health. It took a long time before I could accurately articulate how I felt. I no longer felt anything. Completely and utterly unfeeling. But the odd thing was that I thought things.

Let me explain. It felt like the feelings started out deep down inside me, but as they started to rise, they began to travel through a viscous material, sort of like Jell-O. By the time the feeling broke through the surface, it had lost its 'feeling-ness', and just became a thought. I no longer had any feelings, just thoughts. I no longer felt happy, even though I knew I was. I no longer felt excited, even though I knew I was. It was a very unpleasant state in which to be in. I returned to my doctor and described for him how I was feeling, and how all the other side-effects were not pleasant. He then prescribed yet another anti-depressant to take along with my original one. The one major positive effect it had immediately is that it cured my insomnia.

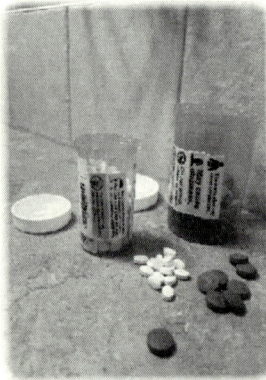

At the beginning, it was wonderful to sleep, and to have the ability to just drop off to sleep like jumping off a cliff ... pure paradise! But then come the dreams. I have always been a vivid dreamer and have had episodes of sleep walking when I was a kid, and according to my wife, I jabber on like a parrot on meth when I sleep. It is not like I suffer what I would call night terrors or even nightmares, but I have very concerning and disturbing dreams. Many of them I wake up in the middle and I find myself swimming in night sweats, but not afraid. I have never had a dream of any nature of incidents that I have experienced... no flashbacks, not even intrusive thoughts or memories. But the dreams are still one of the ongoing issues I must tolerate.

As is common with depression, I really started to notice my flagging cognitive abilities. I have always had a bit of a poor memory, especially for faces (pretty bad for someone who works in law enforcement, eh?). What I found happening, regardless of the medication, was that my memory was very much going down hill, and I still find it difficult to remember some basic things told to me and then immediately forgotten. I will talk more about the cognitive effects of depression later in the section on operational stress injuries.

In general, I continued to struggle with motivation, irritability and paranoia. Regarding the paranoia, during the deeper moments, I had gone out to my patrol car and found some minor parts missing from my computer mount and the end of my cell charging cord was torn off. I was sure that someone had been in my patrol car and had caused this damage. Thankfully, I never made any blatant accusations, and I realized later that each was coincidental and were done innocently by my operation of the vehicle. I continued to withdraw, headaches continued, and I then started finding myself holding my breath. I would just become aware that I was not breathing.

Finally, I sought out the help of a psychologist of my own choosing following my own research. The details of my therapy are not important for the sake of this book, only that it shed some light on some things, and yet did not at the same time on others. One of the things that did stick with me still haunts me.

I shared with my psychologist that I was having problems with *feeling*. I told her that I used to be passionate about things that were important to me, and that I would typically feel physically excited about certain things. I always said that when I sat down to accomplish something regarding curriculum and program design for my company, my muse would descend, and the fire would be lit. I could work for hours. Of course, this could be taken as mania, but I would accomplish so many valuable outcomes. I also explained that this lack of excitement applied to participating in travels, vacations, and holidays. Just nothing there.

After exploring this, no surprise revelations were discovered, and her opinion was that, due to my advancing age, maturity and various impacts of the anxiety and depression disorders, "Maybe this is just the new you." I truly hate writing it down, let alone thinking about it.

I have invested much thought on this point, and still struggle to accept this. The common word most people, especially employers, have used to describe me is *passionate* and it has always been a key descriptor in my self-identity. And now it just is not there. I know I look forward to things, and I know that I still value my accomplishments. I just do not feel the excitement anymore. This makes me very dull in my mind. It makes me wonder if this is just one more unfortunate side effect of the medication I am on, or if it is a permanent scar resulting from the traumas, or just a natural evolution in my psychological and emotional make-up. Either way, I am stuck with a lustreless perspective.

Following my therapy, I felt better about my mental health, without fooling myself that I was mentally well again. I can accept having mental health issues, but I do recall feeling like I could go on being the same first responder I always was. I had attended several collision scenes during all this and did not have any adverse responses. However, shortly thereafter, I attended the scene of a collision involving a semi truck and trailer and a small commercial vehicle. The driver of the commercial truck did not escape the cab and burned with the truck.

The collision occurred prior to my shift starting, and so when I attended to see if there was anything I could do to support the services on-scene, I believed that the scene was just secured for the investigation, and further believed the deceased driver of the commercial vehicle had already been taken from the scene. I was wrong.

There was some activity at the truck cab, and as I looked over they were removing the charred body of the driver. I recall seeing, with wonder, that the one foot was completely intact and was not burned. It appeared to me that the boot must have burned and then went out before the foot could be damaged. The remaining leg was bone covered with scant charred flesh. For the first time ever in my career, my stomach did a barrel roll. I am not, nor have I ever been, nauseous around casualties. As it made quite an impact on me, it was then when I decided that I was going to spare myself anymore adverse reactions. I promised myself that my attendance at future collisions would strictly be traffic control, without attending the actual scene. There... problem solved, right?

Nope. The very next collision I went to happened less that 100 metres from where I had just initiated a traffic stop. I observed the driver of my subject vehicle exit his vehicle, I stepped out of my patrol car. He was pointing in my direction, and when I turned around I saw the carnage. Passenger vehicle versus semi-truck and trailer.

I returned to my vehicle and drove to the scene, calling for back-up. I first turned my attention to the driver of the passenger vehicle. The front end of the vehicle was pushed up into the front passenger area of the vehicle, and the driver was wedged in between his seat and the dashboard. I recall his head was freely bleeding and he had moved as I was trying to assess his consciousness. However, I knew within seconds that he was deceased, and that the movement was strictly a post-mortem twitch. Of course, I was in an area that is notorious for poor radio signal, and that day was no different. I was unable to update responding units. I remember asking about the driver of the semi, and someone pointed him out; he was walking around and talking on the phone. I was informed that he was okay. At one point, a bystander handed me her phone saying she had 9-1-1 on the line. I was able to update dispatch, and then turned my attention back to the vehicle.

To search for other occupants of the passenger vehicle, I smashed the side windows as the seats in the vehicle broke off and were tossed about. Thankfully, I was able to determine there was no other passenger. Shortly thereafter, the bystander returned and handed me the phone again. I was told by dispatch that they had received information that there may have been a one-year-old child occupant in the vehicle. I think that any first responder will know what this did to me on-scene. I completed a more thorough visual of the interior of the vehicle. While I was doing this, the responding units arrived, and took over the scene. They confirmed that the driver was deceased. I offered to remain on scene to provide traffic support, as the highway needed to be shut down. I am still torn as to whether this was the smart choice or the dumb choice.

Once I had a chance to place my patrol vehicle, I called my acting supervisor (our supervisor was away at the time). I found my voice hitchy, and I was on the verge of tears. I found I could barely communicate. My supervisor did a fantastic job in handling me while in crisis, especially since I caught him off duty and sitting down to dinner with my family. I recall trying to use humour to ground myself and told him to "Mental Health First Aid" me. I assured him that I would be okay to stay to assist and asked him to contact my wife as I could barely get any words out. I continued to struggle against the emotional storm I was feeling. A fire truck attended my checkpoint, and as I greeted them, one asked if I was alright. I told him that I was, and he replied, "B---S---! I can hear it in your voice" His crew stayed with me for a moment to ensure I was not going to break down right then, gave me water, and then continued onto the scene.

I feel that staying at the scene may have been a blessing in disguise. I am sure that, on some level, the time I was able to decompress and to process the event. I was able to take advantage of the solitude to do some breathing exercises, and to write my notes for my report. I hope it was processing and not just suppression. After all the years of suppressing stress, I cannot truly tell anymore. I ended up remaining on scene for a few hours and then went home. I did not break down at home, and I felt relatively normal, my new normal. I still have not experienced any adverse experiences from this one yet. But I am much more concerned about my increasingly strong emotional responses. I suspect that this response was predicated by the fact of the surprise factor.

I was completely unprepared for this collision. Even when close to a scene, one can steel himself for the inevitable carnage. Ironically, once making the decision to actively avoid said carnage, fate decided to remind me that it is not up to me.

CHAPTER 6

Exploring Stress Related Disorders

Here, we delve into the world of stress: the physical signs and symptoms, the biological impact and the emotional and social impact of stress and the dysfunctions that follow. I initially titled this chapter "Exploring Operational Stress"... However, I figure that operational stress is pretty much the same as just plain old stress, just that it results from the operational duties that we as first responders do. I just want you to know that this stress can arise from any problematic situation in your life, and operational duties do not generally make these go away. Indeed, they typically will exacerbate them, compounding them and then creating their own symptoms. Sometimes it feels like you just cannot win.

What are the symptoms and signs of stress? I have found that the signs and symptoms of stress, for the purposes of this book, are indicated by the very same signs and symptoms of anxiety and depression. There are numerous signs and symptoms, and they are very diverse in how they are exhibited in the individual. We all experience with individual differences, especially intensity and frequency.

PHYSICAL	
Chronic headache	Flaring of stress related conditions (such as cold sores, psoriasis, eczema, migraine)
Muscle tension (especially neck and shoulders)	Sleep disturbances (too much or too little)
Muscle exhaustion	Eating disturbances (too much or too little)
General aches and pains	Declining personal hygiene
Rapid breathing or holding breath	Fatigue
Trembling/tingling in limbs	Tight chest

MENTAL/EMOTIONAL	
Paranoia	Difficulty with concentration
Lack of motivation	Failing memory
General hypersensitivity	Worsening insomnia
Hypersensitivity to high emotion (eg: soldiers returning home; first responder funerals)	Flattening of emotion
	Concerning dreams/nightmares

BELIEFS	
Useless	Harm is imminent
To blame for everything	Suicide is an option
Irresponsible	Will never get over it
Hindrance to family/friends	Grief
Deserted by higher power	Self-hate

The impact of chronic stress can, and will, have a detrimental effect on the health of the first responder. While I was in university, I recall studies were conducted regarding the physical stress on first responders based on the impact on firefighters of being jolted away by the tones going off while they were asleep, and the impact of shift work on police, the sedentary condition of most police and EMS daily operations, etc. There is so much more known biologically now, that it is difficult to deny those effects. I will leave it up to you to look into healthy lifestyle choices. I will, however, delve into the effects of dousing ourselves in stress chemicals for the long haul, specifically *cortisol, norepinephrine,* and *serotonin.*

We know that marinating our bodies in stress chemicals such as cortisol, norepinephrine, and serotonin has nothing but detrimental effects on our physical health. Although there are some kinds of stress that are beneficial, I prefer to focus on the very stress that creates a state of vulnerability for first responders. I think that the major effect that stress has on first responders arises from its chronic nature.

According to the Dartmouth Undergraduate Journal of Science[3], Michael Randall (2011) writes that cortisol's main function is to restore homoeostasis following exposure to stress. Because chronic stress typically interferes with the return to homoeostasis, the cortisol does not get used in the system, thus remains in the body. Another function of cortisol is that it counters insulin

---

[3] Randall, M. 2011. *The Physiology of Stress: Cortisol and the Hypothalamic-Pituitary-Adrenal Axis* http://dujs. dartmouth.edu/2011/02/the-physiology-of-stress-cortisol-and-the-hypothalamic-pituitary-adrenal-axis/

by encouraging higher blood sugar and the production of glucose. Cortisol carefully regulates the level of glucose circulating through the bloodstream.

Cortisol's weakening effects on the immune response have also been well documented. It's ability to prevent the strengthening of the immune response can render individuals suffering from chronic stress highly vulnerable to infection. Constantly being sick takes its toll on everyone, but it is especially impactful for first responders as we rely on our ability to focus and ignore our own conditions. This can prove slightly more difficult if your sinuses are compromised, or suffering from headache, or constantly coughing or sneezing, not to mention contaminating the people with whom we are dealing. We also face the monster of weight gain and developmental impairment.

Randall continues to link ill effects of the role of cortisol, and how chronic stress impacts memory. The hippocampus, the region of the brain where memories are processed and stored, contains numerous cortisol receptors. When cortisol levels are at normal levels, the hippocampus is not affected adversely. However, excess cortisol overwhelms the hippocampus and actively causes atrophy. Fortunately, the damage incurred is usually not permanent. I have found that my own memory has been significantly impacted by my conditions. I have never really had a great memory, especially for names and faces, but over the last couple of years, I have noticed markedly declining ability to remember basic things.

Typical of first responders, Randall found that stressed Dartmouth students often sacrifice sleep while increasing consumption of caffeine and alcohol, all which impact cortisol levels and thus, the physiological markers of the stress response. Acute sleep loss creates systemic confusion and disrupts regulation of the system. On top of that, repeated doses of caffeine over a single day result in markedly increased cortisol levels, regardless of the stressor involved. A positive relationship appears to exist between caffeine intake and cortisol release, and this relationship is exacerbated when other stressors are introduced. Thus, combining a lack of sleep with multiple cups of coffee or energy drinks reinforces the negative effects of the stress response and further undermines performance.

As first responders, we have the tendency of releasing stress through consumption of liquor. However, alcohol stimulates and encourages the manufacture and release of cortisol. It is not of surprise, then, that first responders suffer from the consequences of considerable anxiety and pressure: our common responses to stress, lack of sleep, caffeine intake, and alcohol consumption act in conjunction to raise the amount of cortisol in our bodies, adding to the very stress we seek to reduce.

According to Randall:

> *"the long-term, constant cortisol exposure associated with chronic stress produces further symptoms, including impaired cognition, decreased thyroid function, and accumulation of abdominal fat, which itself has implications for cardiovascular health. The bottom line is that both episodes of acute stress and more prolonged stressful circumstances precipitate lower levels of general health, and exposure to such stress should be minimized."*

Norepinephrine (noradrenaline) is a more potent type of adrenaline. It gives us the fight or flight response for survival. This instinct does not just relate to physical threat, but emotional as well. Norepinephrine lights the fire for survival: increases heart-rate and respiration, raises blood pressure, heightens the senses, focuses attention, and raises the level of fear. This is all good when it pertains to an immediate threat; however, when it comes to the aftermath of a traumatic experience or cumulation of multiple traumas, it creates problems for mental health. Bremner (2016)[4] reports that norepinephrine is instrumental in the aftermath, as it tends to play a role in sustaining the symptoms of post-traumatic stress disorder, symptoms such as irritability, increased hyper-arousal, and sleep disruptions; therefore, contributing as well to the generalized anxiety and depressive disorders. Like all other chemicals associated with survival, norepinephrine draws resources away from biologic maintenance, and in the long term, processes and structures begin to break down. We see the development of diabetes, hypertension, neurotransmitter malfunctions, gastrointestinal conditions, sleeplessness, slow to heal from injury, and numerous other undesirable conditions.

Serotonin is another neurotransmitter that plays a role in dysfunctions related to chronic stress. An irregular production of serotonin has been associated with depression, anxiety, aggression, impulsivity and suicidal behaviour all of which are frequently found in patients with post-traumatic stress disorder[5].

The clinical signs and symptoms of Post-Traumatic Stress Disorder are described in the Diagnostic and Statistical Manual published by the American Psychiatric Association, revised in 2013, updating the criteria and addition of a chapter in Trauma- and Stressor-Related Disorders. Prior to this revision, PTSD was considered strictly an anxiety disorder. The diagnostic criteria for the manual's new edition[6] identify the trigger to PTSD as exposure to actual or

---

[4] Bremner, J.D. (2016) *Post-traumatic Stress Disorder*. John Wiley & Sons, Hoboken, New Jersey.

[5] Canadian Medical Association (1997) *Post-traumatic Stress Disorder and Serotonin: New Directions for Research and Treatment*. Review Paper

[6] American Psychiatric Association. 2013. "Post Traumatic Stress Disorder" Fact Sheet.

threatened death, serious injury or sexual violation. The exposure must result from one or more of the following scenarios, in which the individual:

- directly experiences the traumatic event;
- witnesses the traumatic event in person;
- learns that the traumatic event occurred to a close family member or close friend (with the actual or threatened death being either violent or accidental) or
- experiences first-hand repeated or extreme exposure to aversive details of the traumatic event (not through media, pictures, television or movies unless work-related)

At least one of the following	
Intrusive thoughts or images of the event	Distress when reminded of event
Dreams or nightmares about the event or similar events	Physical arousal (becoming physically upset) when reminded of event
Flashbacks or illusions about the event (children may act out event in play)	

At least one of the following	
Avoidance of thoughts or feelings associated with the event	Avoidance of reminders of the trauma (people, places, activities, objects or situations)

At least two of the following	
Inability to recall important aspects of event (not explained by loss of consciousness)	Persistent negative trauma related emotions (eg: fear, horror, anger, guilt or shame)
Ongoing negative beliefs and expectations about oneself (eg: "I am bad") or the world	Decreased interest in previously significant/ enjoyable activities
"The world is a very dangerous place"	Feeling detached/alienated from others
Unnecessarily blaming self or others for causing the event or for consequences	Restricted emotions (eg: persistent inability to experience positive emotions)

At least two of the following	
Irritable or aggressive behaviour	Exaggerated startle response (too easily startled or scared)
Self-destructive or careless behaviour	Difficulty concentrating
Hyper-vigilance (always on guard)	

Additional Criteria	
Symptoms last for more than one month	Symptoms create distress or functional impairment (eg: social, occupations)
Symptoms are not due to medication, substance use or other illness	

As we have discovered, the stress of everyday life, let alone the life of the first responder, can lead to serious disruptions of physical and mental health. We can all attest to the stressors we encounter daily; however, I can speak to the impact of when that stress becomes acute. I have suffered the onslaught of bodily pain and injury due to my depression and anxiety. I have also fought demons in my mind that were causing my withdrawal from everything that is important to me. Kind of hard to do when you consider that it is impossible to just will your body to produce or suppress neurotransmitters. Medications can do this, but my experience has been that there tends to be unattractive side-effects. It basically comes down to which is the lesser of two evils. I choose my relatively stable moods and ability to sleep over the less than pleasant side effects of the medications I currently take.

CHAPTER 7

Working from Inside Out: Brain, Body & Behaviour

This portion of the session will involve learning about emotional intelligence, and how the brain and the central nervous system impact how we respond emotionally to the environment around us. How we respond to psychological and emotional threat is not set in stone, as neuroplasticity allows us to shape our responses. I have often heard, especially from me, that our brains are our worst enemies.

Change is not as simple as I believed it to be. I always thought the changes I made in my life were ultimately simple just because I did not have to expend much conscious effort on them. Remember the ability to see the forest through the trees? I have known the concepts of neuroplasticity and the ways of neural pathway development for years. But never had I had to embrace truly how difficult it will be for me to kindle new pathways. I know that strong emotional events kindle thick neural pathways and make it harder to reformulate different pathways. It's something I must continually work on. In this chapter, we will learn the how and why, and how to get back at them!

We will start with cognition. Cognition is simply the way we acquire, store, transform and use information[7]. These are the basic structures that will illustrate why operational stress can impact so much on our physical bodies and our behaviour. Neurons are nerve cells that are responsible for transmitting information, in the form of neurotransmitters, from Point A to Point B. Stress and brain injuries can, and do, affect how effectively our brains can transfer and process information as it comes in, how information is sensed and perceived, stored and recalled. It is also how our

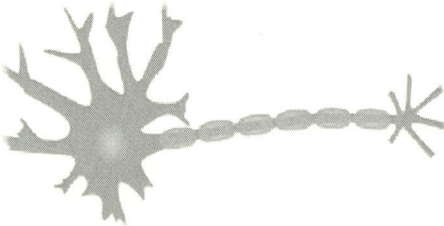

---

[7] Matlin, M. (2013) *Cognition*, 8th Ed. John Wiley & Sons, Inc. Hoboken, NJ

information filters through certain brain structures that involve emotion, memory, and our survival instincts.

Information is encoded into chemicals (neurotransmitters), and using electrical pulses, this information flows from one neuron to another. Neural pathways are simply the strings of neurons that carry out specific functions. There is no need, for the purpose of this book, to learn how to be a biologist to combat operational stress. The intended purpose of this section is to demonstrate how the body can conspire against us, and how to use science to reprogram our brains to do what *we* want *them* to do, not the other way around. Neurotransmitters are released from the end of one neuron to the next, as illustrated in the diagram.

In a process called neuronal re-uptake, the neurotransmitters are then essentially absorbed into the receiving neuron, and sent along the path through the neuron to the other end, and the process repeats itself. Why is this important to understand? When we have chemical imbalances in our bodies, these neurotransmitters may not be produced, or may be flawed, or over produced. For example, while there is a controversy over the role of serotonin uptake processes regarding depression and anxiety, the currently accepted thought is that depression and anxiety are affected by low levels of serotonin.

Common medications for these conditions are selective serotonin re-uptake inhibitors (SSRI), which after a ton of science-y explanations, provides for more serotonin to be usable by the brain. Research has shown that the *stress chemical* cortisol can impact the production of serotonin[8], reducing it and creating an imbalance; thus, exacerbating the problem and possibly leading to the need for medication.

So now that we have covered the basics of neural transmission, we will look at how our brains can be the enemy. At the basic level, the brain's complexity is astonishing. The human brain is an amazing structural marvel, a well evolved, but very old, muscle.

First, we will discuss the very basic brain structure we have. The brain stem is what ultimately keeps us alive. This structure plays a key role in regulation of our cardiac and respiratory systems, pumping the heart and bringing oxygen into the system. It also plays a pivotal role in maintaining consciousness and regulating sleep, as well as eating. Of course, there are many other processes the brain stem manages, and the interplay between the brain

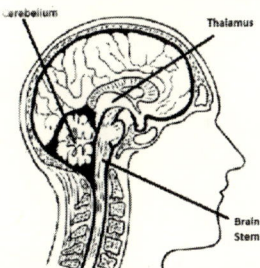

[8] Tafet, Toister-Achituv, & Shinitzky. (2001). *Correlation Between Cortisol Level and Serotonin Uptake in Patients with Chronic stress and Depression*. National Center for Biotechnology Information [Abstract].

stem and the rest of the brain is very multifaceted, but for anyone who has suffered even the most minor stress, you will know how our basic functions are impacted. Here are just some of the symptoms of stress, generalized anxiety disorder (GAD) and depression[9]:

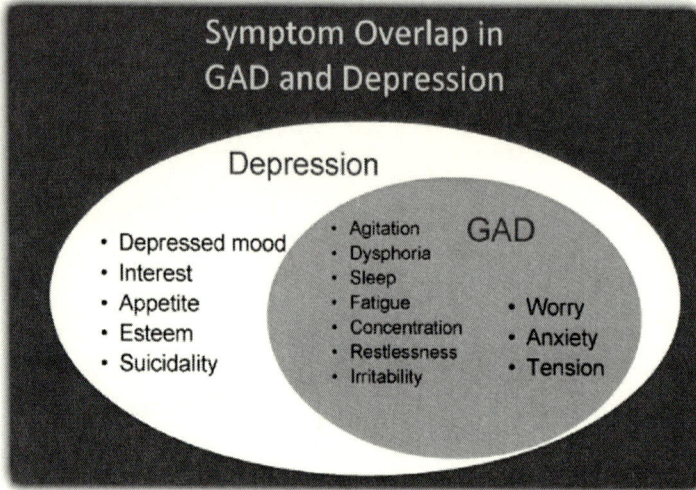

Some of us cannot eat when stressed out, perhaps suffering upset stomach or indigestion, and then others stress-eat. Sleep disruption is a very common sign of mental health issues, either too much (depression) or too little (anxiety). Ultimately, however, the brain stem is responsible for keeping us physically alive.

Next, we are going to go far back during our early cave man days, and discuss the lizard brain, also know as the mid-brain. The lizard brain refers to the functions of the mid-brain, structures such as the amygdala, thalamus and cerebellum. These structures regulate emotion, behaviour, motivation and arousal, addiction, and long-term memory, among many other functions. The thalamus and cerebellum primarily are information relay structures, and will participate in how we manage fear and stress in our lives. The amygdala is a small structure that is a storehouse of emotional memory. Consider this non-threatening situation:

You are walking in a park and you spot an apple tree. Your brain recognizes, through sensations in your stomach and the recognition of the apple as food, that you are hungry. Of course, survival requires you to be cautious, so you look around for hazards before approaching the tree: are there snakes, hungry leopards, poisonous man-eating plants, or dinosaurs drowning in tar pits near the tree? Nope. Ok. So, you approach the tree and look for a safe apple. Is there acid dripping from the fruit nearest to you? Is there a snake slithering out of the

[9] Roy-Byrne PP, Katon W.J Clin *Psychiatry*. 1997; 58 (suppl 3):34-38; discussion 39-40

fruit? Is there a leopard hiding on the branch waiting for an unsuspecting apple eater? Nope. Ok. Is it, in fact, an apple? Yes, you recognizethe apple because you have eaten apples in the past. And they did not kill you, so you are safe there.

Since your hunger is still there, and you remember liking the taste of apples, you reach out and pick the apple and then you eat it. All this assessment happens relatively quickly as far as brain processing is concerned. Biologically speaking, the amygdala has the potential to be a down and dirty survival mechanism, and has the ability to interrupt the information relay to the neocortex, where the executive functions of the brain take place. This interruption, referred to by Daniel Goleman in his book *Emotional Intelligence* as an *amygdala hijack*[10], responds to a threatening condition in the environment and, for time's sake, prevents the information from being slowly processed by the neocortex.

Goleman writes that the old theory of threat recognition and response held that information came in through the senses, was sent to the relay structures, disseminated to all the relevant structures for interpretation, and once the threat was adequately analyzed, action would result. However, in the mid 1980s, a neuroscientist named Joseph LeDoux located a new neural pathway that wired the amygdala directly to the thalamus. This new pathway provided evidence that there was a quicker, dirtier, process involved when immediate threats are detected. According to this approach, the thalamus receives the information and it is now sent to the amygdala at the same time as it is being sent to the visual cortex. This allows the amygdala instead to signal the body's survival instincts to kick in and responds much faster before the true nature of the threat is fully consciously recognized.

As Goleman's diagram from his book shows, when we encounter a threat, and we sense it (in this case, we SEE thesnake), this sensory information is first filtered through the thalamus. The thalamus will then relay this information to the visual cortex (as this is the part of the brain that interprets visual stimuli), and will then transmit the information to the amygdala and to the rest of the brain responsible for interpreting the information. The amygdala very quickly compares this information with its internal memory (long-term) and verifies that HOLY CRAP! A SNAKE! MOVE! and then

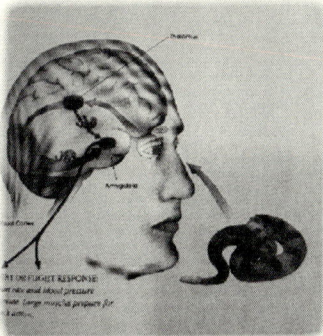

---

[10] Goleman, D. (1995). *Emotional Intelligence: Why It Can Matter More than IQ*. New York, New York. Bantam Dell.

sends that information directly to the central nervous system causing the body to ramp up its sympathetic nervous system to dump adrenalin into the system, draw more oxygen into the system, vasodilate to prevent circulation issues on the surface, among other process, and to ultimately cause you to move away from the threat, all the while the info is still moving through the cognitive processes that take so much more time.

How does this apply to our behaviour? The exact same way as it does for when we encounter a physical threat. When was the last time you lost your temper, and before you knew to stop, you either struck out physically or verbally

toward someone? If you had not been taken by surprise or mad angry, would you have still responded so? We see this in the first responder world, and not just from ourselves or our colleagues when suffering mental illness and are abnormally agitated. As a law enforcement officer, I see people lose their minds roadside. Where did their amygdala hijacks start? Probably when they saw the emergency lights come on. Immediately, their sympathetic nervous system activates. Why? What is the threat?

It could be one of many things: driver cannot afford another ticket, there is something to hide in the vehicle, the driver is not a fan of cops, prior negative experiences in similar circumstances, or any number of unknowns. And when the sympathetic nervous system activates, it triggers the amygdala. I have always said that if you want to turn an honest person into a liar, put him behind the steering wheel of a vehicle. In that circumstance, it is the lie told to the officer that is the amygdala hijack: lie to protect one's self. It is usually the first response out of the mouth, likely more of a knee jerk reaction. This demonstrates how amygdala hijacks affect our behaviour, not only when confronting physical danger, but also psychological or emotional danger. This is a rapid way of turning on emotions, as the cells are fast, but they are not very precise and tend to cause exaggerated responses.

Of course, the process of neural transmission, the brain's processing of information, and how we respond is more complex than what is written here, it very basically demonstrates how information from the outside world affects our brains, and therefore our bodies, and our behaviour as well.

So, all of that explains how our brains work without real thought or conscious analysis of the information coming from all around us. Next, we will look at how we can assert control over our thought processes and work toward optimizing how we respond to the functioning of our neocortex. The neocortex holds our higher executive functioning, also referred to as the mammalian brain. Our neocortex makes us uniquely human, in that it provides our capacity to comprehend the abstract, to problem-solve, and perceive the world around us. The neocortex is located between your temples and is made up of all the wrinkly parts of your outer brain. The neocortex is divided into lobes: frontal lobe, parietal lobe, occipital lobe and the temporal lobe. These lobes carry on the processes of our ability to analyze and not just respond, unless engaged in an amygdala hijack.

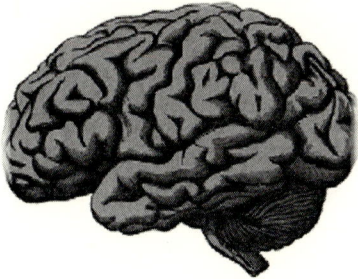

To use our brains to our advantage, to act like mammals and not lizards, we need to work toward proficient control over our brains. Cognitive processing can take place both in a bottom-up fashion or a top-down fashion. Bottom-up processing is virtually demonstrated by the limbic system, as eventually the event will come to the higher ups to compartmentalize everything and break it all down, and then make a decision that has already been made. However, using our higher functioning structures of the brain to figure things out is top-down processing.

Consider bottom-up and top-down leadership. This is no different. When the grunts lead from the trenches, we see immediate life-saving decision making without significant pause. However, as we know, the top-down leadership demonstrates timely analysis of any given situation, and when an instant decision is required, those in the trenches tend to suffer for it. If we are not truly in danger, we can engage these brain functions to control the world around us in a top-down process; thus, exercising control over our lives and our thoughts and emotions. If you have ever taken any course on mental health, operational stress injuries, or just stress management, you will know that control is everything. Loss of personal control is central to many mental disorders and can be alleviated to some degree simply by asserting control over the environment.

One of the more central brain structures that will assist us in this endeavour is the hippocampus. The hippocampus plays a role in emotions; it has a keen memory for context and makes sense of perception. As you will see, the hippocampus is important for us in relation to our ability to correctly identify threats. For example, it helps us recognize the differing significance of a bear in the zoo as opposed to a bear in your backyard. To manage our emotions and our responses to threats and/or regular stress, we must consider how the brain works before we can play around with it. We must be able to ensure the appropriateness of emotions and knowing what an appropriate response in a threatening situation is. Emotional situations can be looked at as dangerous, but they are not life threatening, and by recognizing this, we can take the time to determine appropriateness.

CHAPTER 8

Emotional Intelligence: Finding the Real You

Emotional intelligence was posited in the 1980s in an article by John Mayer and Peter Salovey, and further researched by a psychologist named Daniel Goleman[11]. This approach to intelligence came about in direct opposition to the *intelligence quotient* (IQ) system of evaluating intelligence. IQ was found to be limited in its effectiveness in predicting success in life. There were people in the world, extremely intelligent to IQ standards, but they could not hold a social situation to save their lives. Goleman was interested in why that was, and how to harness other qualities that would help people increase their ability to expand the status quo concept of intelligence. Some criticize the validity of emotional intelligence as a predictor of corporate and/or organizational success[12], I accept emotional intelligence as a construct on which to build personal success and present it as such in my First Few Steps programs. I firmly believe that you cannot lead others until you can lead yourself. While I do not completely believe that emotional intelligence is the cure for organizational malaise, a person who exercises effective control through the development and practice of the concepts of emotional intelligence can, and should, succeed.

Growing up, I wish I would have had this framework in my head. While I was good in school, my brother was not, and I never grasped the conflict that this would cause when I spoke about how school was easy. I also used to lie like a rug. I told lies for all the regular reasons: deflect blame, afraid of getting in trouble, personal gain and so on. I also had some sticky fingers. That is all you get for disclosure from me, as I already went through all that ancient history when applying for police jobs in my earlier years.

The point here is that these behaviours and mindsets would have dire consequences when I entered the workforce. Had I known better, I could have saved myself a lot of grief. However, I was fortunate to have undergone a

---

[11] Goleman, D. (1995). *Emotional Intelligence: Why It Can Matter More than IQ*. New York, New York. Bantam Dell.

[12] Lindebaum, D. (2009) "Rhetoric or Remedy? A Critique on Developing Emotional Intelligence", *Academy of Management Learning & Education*, 2009, Vol. 8, No. 2, 225–237.

transformation and eventually was able to address most of these concerns, all before learning about emotional intelligence.

I made mention of the difficulties I experienced in my marriage at the beginning of the book. These difficulties were truly the beginning of my journey into self-development. I recall being very unhappy, with how my life was progressing and how my marriage was not helping me be satisfied. Communication was a problem between my wife and I, first and foremost. We had two polar opposite ways of dealing with conflict, and I found out later that my way had more of a profound effect on my wife than hers did on me. Since it bears much on the discussion of stress management for first responders, I will relay my old way of resolving personal and inner conflict. I always believed that I had some magic pressure valve deep down inside. I must have, because I do not ever remember really getting angry about anything. When I did get stressed, all I needed to do was shut my mouth to ensure I did not say anything I would regret, remove myself from the situation, and after a bit of time, it would just all go POOF! All gone! Or so I thought. Remember the chickens roosting chapter?

It turns out that this style was not congruent with my wife's experience. I learned later than someone in my wife's life used to act the same way but done in a manner to punish her. Even though this was not my intention, it did nothing to improve our relationship. A side note on self talk. This has become a strategy for many to touch base with yourself and to work through mental issues. However, for me, it has been nothing but cancerous. I would have arguments with people, primarily my wife, in my head. I felt I knew my wife so well, that I knew how she responds and how she thinks, so I could magically speak for her, so to speak. I would have these arguments all day and then come home in either of two conditions: angrier that when it all started because I had worked my way into a tizzy, or calm because the argument had been settled already… in my head.

In either case, my wife either was taken by surprise by the extent of my anger, or still mad and now angrier at me. I finally had to make a concerted effort to literally stop what I was doing, tell myself to STOP, and make myself relax and divert my thoughts. There were a lot of other factors involved in those early years; however, my goal here is to discuss the moment of clarity, as fuzzy as it was for me. I cannot remember the very day my fuzzy moment of clarity happened, but I do remember that it was finally strong enough to compel me to internalize the fact that I can only change what is wrong with me.

Around this time, I was given some advice by my manager at the time. I was always a "rager" against the machine and was having difficulty controlling my frustration at work over what I thought was wrong. It was not the first time I had heard this, but he told me not to worry about those things that were out of my control. It did not really make an impact then, but it certainly proved to be a gem. It would be years before I took that advice, but it still plays a role in me keeping my sanity to this very day. I moved on shortly thereafter to what I thought was going to be my break-out job, but once again, big let down. However, what it did was give me the chance to step out of my comfort zone and stand up for myself. Except that I overcompensated, and I traded door mat for sharing without concern for office politics. This mixed with inept management and even more inept personalities, and I nuked my bridges.

Just in the interest of catharsis, let me tell of a few examples that illustrate the conditions in which I worked. I worked for a start-up company. As is always the case with start-ups, the marketing of this new company was that it was better than all the rest, as they were dedicated to top notch human resources and professional training. I had submitted a few small proposals for ideas I had that would help grow the company, and I began to feel that these proposals were not welcome. I was beginning to get that same feeling about the training programs I was developing. I was hired to be the trainer and was a certified instructor for several programs. I was in the middle of training a certified program, and an errand arose. This errand could have been handled by any one of four people in the office, but I, the certified instructor, was taken out of my class to carry out this errand and was replaced by my supervisor, not a certified instructor. This particular incident, however, was not an isolated incident. So much for dedicated to professional training for staff.

The final straw for me was working on a proposal to create a training school within the company. I researched the legislation and process to ensure it was logistical and economically feasible. In the resulting proposal, I demonstrated how lucrative the endeavour could be (annual income in the six figures at minimum), how we would benefit from offering employment to the top graduates, and how this would bring us in line with the marketing promises we were failing to meet. We would receive tuition from students so there would be a profit margin to add to the company coffers.

Around the time I completed the proposal, the company had engaged the services of a business consultant to conduct an organizational review of the company. He was formerly a military logistics expert now working in the private sector. I asked him if he would review my proposal and would welcome his professional opinion. When he returned it, he asked me if I had served with the military. I informed him that I had not, and he surprised me by telling me that my proposal was written in the same manner as he had written proposals in the military. He then told me of his support for such an endeavour. I did not disclose that I had the consultant review the proposal. When I submitted it to my supervisor, he briefly glanced at the cover and ask me "Why do you keep wasting my time with these?" and tossed the proposal into the garbage can. Shortly thereafter, the company beat me to the punch and terminated me... well, laid me off... but we all knew the truth. In my termination letter, they said that the consultant had recommended the dissolution of my position, as it was based upon the retention of a particular contract, and the contract was no longer. Of course, the company was making loads of money at the time, and could have supported my position, oh and ... they were not aware of my lengthy conversations with the consultant. If I can at least take some petty satisfaction, the company did not last much longer. Should have listened to me.

Why am I telling you these stories? Am I petty and pouty? Well, I am, kind of. But here I want to set up why I felt I needed to rethink my professional style, as well as my personality. So, I began to look at self-help books to explore the problem. The first self-help book I read was "Don't Sweat the Small Stuff". I got through the first few pages and threw it in the garbage. First time I ever threw a book away. It did not help at all for this rager against the machine. I needed a more powerful aggressive approach to making me a better person. This is when I finally became aware of emotional intelligence. I began to read about this framework, and I remember thinking, "Wow! This is me!". It showed me the path that I had already started and provided more of a plan going forward. It really helped get through my first challenges in law enforcement, both in terms of working with the public and later working with a difficult partner.

Since first responders work intimately with their respective teams, and more so when working directly with a partner, it is vital that they are capable of self management of stresses and the rougher edges of their personalities. I have worked with some of the best people on this planet over the years, but I have also, unfortunately, worked with those who emotional intelligence was completely non-existent.

This can be the deal breaker when it comes to loyalty to an employer, as it became one of a couple deal breakers for me. Nothing is worse than having to spend so much time in close confines as a patrol car with someone that really you cannot find some common ground on which to teeter on at least. I have worked with people that were two-faced to such a degree that even I was shocked to hear of the extent of that person's treachery. I am very thankful, in that situation, that my reputation saved me with my employer, but with my colleagues my association with this person was very damaging. I worked with one person who, when he found out I was planning on starting to become a trainer, said to me "What makes you think you can teach?". The manner in which it was said certainly did not communicate an honest inquiry into my skills to advance learning. I have been called arrogant and egotistical and have been walked all over. I was the original doormat.

The irony of my maiden voyage to become a trainer was that I had decided that I would no longer be a doormat. I understood that the reason why people treated me that way was because, being the awesome trainer I already knew I was, I allowed them... or in other words... I trained them to do it. Take that, Mr. "What makes you think you can teach?"! I thought that if I could finally just take risks and voice my opinions, I would get the respect of my employers.

Do you know, ultimately, what got me the respect of my employer once I found the right one? Honesty and ethics. It was that simple, kind of serendipitous, really. My employer had recently terminated the previous officer for cause, and my style was the exact opposite. Since I had spent so long being micromanaged, I would run by her everything I was planning to do for the shift, and I think I finally frustrated her enough to get testy with me for the first time.

One day, she finally said to me that I was the expert, now just go out there and do my job. Hallelujah! Yes, ma'am! It was the start of a great relationship. We will look at the power of reputation later, but I feel that this was the one major factor that led to success during my first law enforcement position; however, the planets were aligned for that to happen as significantly as it did. I had the right size of community, the right citizenry for the most part, and the right coworkers and colleagues, for the most part.

In law enforcement, and I suspect in any job, reputation can be a make or break characteristic. Inculcating an environment of trust and benefit of the doubt can, and will, save you countless headaches. There is little worse than always having to explain yourself and defend your actions in every single incident, especially when you are not present to do so. I worked for a person who acted like momma bear with her cubs when it came to staff. It was definitely a breath of fresh air, but I worked hard to create that environment. And I am here to tell you that being honest when you make mistakes, especially the stupid ones, is not an easy task. But then again, what makes things valuable is the very effort it takes to create them.

Yet another experience was working on a team when there was such a personality difference. I was the new guy, and feeling comfortable with the people on my team, I relaxed and was myself. Big mistake. Within a very short time, I found that I had alienated pretty much the entire team. As an aside, when you have been faced with the question "What would you do in the event of a conflict with a co-worker?" I can virtually predict your answer. Why? Because it is the most commonly asked question in interviews, and I have asked and been asked that question numerous times. Let me consult my crystal ball... and your answer would be... I would first address the conflict with that co-worker... blah blah blah. We answer that way because it is the right response. Not the truth, but the right response.

What I can also tell you is that this answer is one of the biggest lies told during interviews. My sense of humour is fairly critical, as I play off on people's strengths and playfully put myself over them, and many other times it is self-depreciating. I have no issue making fun of myself. I recall on more than one occasion, having a closed door talk with a new supervisor, and learned that I had offended my teammates. Seriously, it should never had gone past the first time, especially considering I had apologized after finding out about these events, and even explained my sense of humour and that I highly respected them. This is a shared area of concern in most teams, if not all.

One thing I do often have to ask myself, and I encourage others to do the same, is to ask, "Is it me?". If there is conflict or awkwardness between me and others, I am not so egotistical as to believe I can do no wrong. I have periodically offended people without ever intending to do so due to my free-flowing sense of humour, which some do not appreciate. Even though I have been told that I cannot shoulder all the responsibility for the inter-team conflict, I must consider that this is a common occurrence for me and that I am the common denominator. Therefore, I definitely play a significant role in creating this conflict. I try to hold that in front of me when I face troubles in the workplace. It was my goal to try to get ahead of this to improve my working environment; however, as you have read earlier, around this time, my mental health tanked again, and this time it changed me fundamentally.

The basic structure of emotional intelligence involves self-awareness, self-management, social awareness and social skills. These are the primary factors I consider when it comes to applying emotional intelligence to self-development. I want focus on Self-Awareness and Self-Management, and to break these down individually and provide examples that will hopefully demonstrate their values. When I first came across emotional intelligence, it

resonated with me because it was the path I had already begun, and it provided me with some guidance to where I was hoping to go.

Self-Awareness

Look to yourself for guidance. As I discuss in my leadership program "The First Few Steps", self-awareness is key to life in all aspects. The ability to be in tune with "you" and what is truly going on in your head and your heart is integral to all things mental health. Only you know what is truly bothering you, and even if you do not actually know what it is that is bothering you, honest self-reflection on the matter will help lead you to the cause of your concern. Wilheim Wundt, the father of modern psychology, was the first to hold that introspection could give us insights into the self and ultimately explain our behaviour in a scientific manner. Well, the scientific manner to today's standard does not support the role of introspection, but it plays a significant role on the emotional intelligence platform.

When I finally chose to begin the path to change, the very first struggle I had was self-awareness. I did not think I was engaging in self-deception and I certainly do not believe that I was engaging in self-betrays, the two most common de-railers of one's emotional life. What I did find was that I had a problem with just facing the truth of experiencing stress, conflict, or just plain old anger. During the process, I went from starting out with "venting" it without having to consciously doing it, to "processing". I believed that trying to calm myself, that I was processing, but now I know it for what is was, suppression of my anger. Processing does not equal suppression. Hence my chickens coming home to roost. All I was doing during my processing phase was just isolating myself for longer periods of time. The key was to start being honest with myself and calling a spade a spade. I needed to acknowledge my emotions as they truly were, positive and negative. It is still a skill I struggle with now.

Self-awareness is in some ways very simple, and by simple I do not mean easy, I mean not complex. Self-awareness, in Goleman's words, is "an ongoing attention to one's internal states". Sounds simple enough, no? It certainly is not complex. However, it certainly is not easy. As I wrote earlier, honest is hard. Honesty with someone who can be deceived is easier, though, than being honest with yourself, who truly cannot be deceived by you, unless traumatized. We are not talking about memory suppression to save one's sanity, but just being one with our emotions day to day. Accurate self-awareness is key. To ensure the accuracy of your awareness, you will need to conduct some sort of

self-assessment. You can either figure out a way to accomplish this yourself, or you can follow this basic emotional audit.

What am I feeling?

Feeling is the more primal, raw emotions that we feel, some more instinctual (remember the role the amygdala plays in the hijack?), and some are the more higher functioning emotions. Either way, we should know ourselves well enough to be able to put a name to the way we feel at any given time.

What am I thinking?

Thinking about what we are thinking is called meta-cognition, and it involves our awareness of our thought processes. Knowing what we're thinking helps frame how we are feeling, the legitimate reason why we are feeling that way, and even the ability to know how to respond to that emotion, rather than just approaching emotions from the instinctive level.

What do I want?

At times, we emotionally respond in a manner that does not go over well with the people around us because something is lacking. But even more significantly, asking yourself this allows you to give context to the emotions and thoughts you are having over an event. However, the most significant question you should ask yourself at this juncture is whether or not you actually want to be angry, frustrated, sad, defeated, or whatever else you feel or think at any given time. If the answer is no,

How am I getting in my own way?

This is huge. We all get in our own ways. A weak person strictly blames others. It takes courage to admit that we may be sabotaging our own paths. Knowing we are getting in our way is one thing but understanding how and figuring out a solution that prevents it from happening further is another.

What do I need to do differently?

Here is the crux of the matter; what answering the other questions in the emotional audit will accomplish. Once we know that we are feeling a certain way, and we have an opportunity to analyze the feelings and what we know about it, to ensure what we need out of this and ensuring that we have prevented our self-sabotaging, what are we going to do about it?

However, another key here is to conduct this emotional audit by looking yourself in the mirror. When you DO look in the mirror, make sure you look yourself in the eye! No one will hold you accountable in this process if you do not. This is where self-confidence comes into play. If you sincerely wish to move forward, you must have the confidence in yourself. If you feel like you do not deserve this improvement, you do not feel you deserve to be happy, or you think you are not strong enough to accomplish this goal, you will not succeed. Knowing one's own emotions, recognizing a feeling for what it truly is at the time it is happening to or for you.

Emotional intelligence is the ability to put our internal emotional processes to work for us in the world around us. We do not work within a vacuum, and our emotional awareness will contribute to our success as leaders of either ourselves and/or others.

Motivating oneself is one of the most significant issues surrounding personal growth. Without it, we will accomplish absolutely nothing. Lack of motivation due to laziness is certainly a personality weakness, but how about a lack of motivation based upon mental disorders? One of the struggles I experience still today involves motivation. For example, one of my issues is anxiety; at times, I feel like I must get up and do something, but in a very undirected manner. I recently underwent this maddening situation, and I found myself pacing in the house, knowing that I could study for my university course I am taking, or I could work on this book, or go for a walk, or a myriad of other activities. I just could not motivate myself to do anything, even in the face of the anxiety driving me to do anything.

Motivation is marshaling emotions in the service of a goal; thus, a goal must be identified. This requires a conscious identification of a task and determining an outcome. It also involves the suppression of impulsiveness and delaying gratification, especially if the goal is difficult to attain or requires a significant amount of time. Beside laziness, and lack of ability to select a task, many lose motivation because of feel of failure. If you realize that failure does not guarantee that the task is not accomplish-able, you must motivate yourself more so after failing to continue.

Mistaking what motivates us will motivate others and vice versa is a trap that many of us will fall into. In organizational leadership, this becomes an issue when a manager believes that what motivates him will motivate the workers. We know that this is not always correct, and when it is, it is more of a synchronous environment than most. More realistically, leaders should look to what motivates the workers, regardless of his own motivation. When this trap applies to the individual, I would warn you to beware

of using what motivates others. I know of a person who blamed his parents for all of his emotional issues. When he became an adult, he struggled to identify what those issues were, and struggled to pin a label on them in order to seek out help specific to his issues. I saw him identify with those who were also struggling, but from different issues.

For example, he had a roommate who was the son of an alcoholic. His roommate attended Al-Anon, a support organization for those who currently or in the past live with alcoholism through association with an alcoholic. He decided, because there was alcoholism in his family in the past (his parents broke the cycle prior to his birth), he began internalizing the signs and symptoms more common with this condition, when it was not addressing his issues, in his opinion. His association with this organization and its philosophies did nothing, and he then abandoned it and began looking for the next new group of troubled people with whom to identify. It is vital that we look within to determine what will motivate us, and exercise caution when looking to others for theirs.

Must consider short and long-term motivation, as well as changing motivations as we progress through our lives, and specifically our first responder career. You must learn to leave your comfort zone, as your comfort zone is not necessarily the best place. This can pertain to the many steps of the path to getting support and ultimately help when it all falls apart. Do not let fear stop you. What we typically see in the first responder community is fear as a motivating force, rather than self-preservation. We need to change this. Motivation must come from within and promote survival. Our own bodies set the stage. If our bodies instinctively prepare the body to fight or flee, why can we not apply our higher evolved brains to do so when our emotional and mental wellbeing is at risk?

What I find is a true mystery is that, in this day and age, why anyone can be afraid to reach out to a trusted colleague or friend when that person is in pain, and vice versa, when we know that a colleague is suffering in silence and for whatever reason, chooses not to broach the subject. We must learn and practice the motivation to take care of our own suffering, and in the first responder community, that means taking care of the guy next to you, regardless of the colour of lights on your work vehicle.

Positivity is an absolute necessity to bolster your motivation. As I have written, I struggle with negativity. It was no different when, one Christmas holiday, while I was spending the holiday with my parents. One day, I found myself in a department store. Within seconds, I had already had enough. People staring at their cell phones as they walked in the crowd and not where they were going, people stopping in the aisle with carts blocking the way, people not attempting to do their part to move aside when approaching others... you know the drill if you have ever walked into a box store a week away from Christmas.

And yet, that day, I spent a couple hours in another mall (albeit in a different city) and I realized something that got me thinking. Are you ready for the big reveal...? I am a judgemental cynic. No... really... I am! I know how hard it is to believe. But it is true. I tend to judge people for the boneheaded things I see and experience. While I was at the mall, I was engaged in my typical thought processes for such an environment. I was remembering the department store from the previous sojourn into the pre-Christmas herd, and had it in my head to expect the same.

However, this is not what happened. Oddly enough, I had the exact opposite experience. Yes, I was a bit aggravated due to the typical slow-walkers, but it is expected to encounter this species in such an environment. But when I was in the washroom washing my hands, a guy slightly older than I was looking for paper towels. I had noticed that there was a stack right next to my sink and informed him. He joked about something, and thanked me. He then began to walk through the exit and nearly bowled over a janitor coming in. He sincerely apologized, joked with the janitor, and he left. I was right behind him. As we came around the corner, he nearly collided with another person walking around the corner. He laughed, and I joked with him about not getting out of here alive.

How does a trip to the bathroom at a mall and watching a stranger plow through the crowd like a bulldozer change one's perspective? Positive thinking. As I said, I am a judgemental cynic. I can blame being so jaded on my exposure to the typical negative people at work as a first responder, or due to the fact that

I have dealt with less than respectable people in my personal life, or on the fact that I am the father of three daughters, or whatever. The point is... continuing such a cancerous path, that of negative thinking, is a conscious choice, as is most of our life issues. We choose, for many reasons, to continue to practice behaviours that are not good for us, our spouses and significant others, our children, our employers and colleagues, or for our respective clientele. We just have to make the conscious effort to catch ourselves engaging in the behaviours we want to change, and just switch gears.

I know this sounds a little simplistic and unrealistic. I believe in my heart (and in my brain) that many maladaptive behaviours are, indeed, outside of our conscious control, such that a simple book from me will not help. These are not to what I am referring. I am referring to things that we choose to do because of ego, because of comfort or familiarity, and/or because of habit. I am writing this, and advocating the conscious decision to change our behaviours, based upon the fact that it is exactly what I did, and that it is a possibility for you because I did it, and it worked. I finally recognized the pull of gravity from the precipice at which my marriage was balancing. I made the conscious effort to say "Stop." That was it... just "Stop." Eventually, I began to work on my communication skills and my acceptance that life just was not going to alter itself without any active participation from this guy! And it did not work just for the short term, but I've been able to sustain it over the years.

Sure, I still find myself falling into my bad habits, but I am able to catch myself, and stop myself from taking it further. We just have to recognize that we are thinking or feeling whatever it is that is not working for us, and just say "Stop." Not yell "STOP!!" and insert a primal scream. Just recognize the thought, tell ourselves to stop, and choose the positive alternative. Again, it may sound like I am minimizing the effort that it will take, but I am not. It really was not an effortless process... it took much work on my part to reinvent myself (how I process conflict, how I express my emotions, and how to effectively communicate them to others). All I am saying is that if we do it often enough, and we truly buy into the process, and we truly want to change our perspective, eventually we will evolve the process into habit, only tending to lean to the positive rather than the negative.

I did that at this mall... I opened my eyes and actively looked for the positive, the good, the healthy. And you know what? I saw it everywhere I looked. And I vowed to remind myself when I find myself thinking negatively to "Stop.", and then look around with my new perspective and seek out that one more example of positive to counteract the one more example of negative.

Self-Management

The management of emotions is, by far, the trickiest thing to manage. We have grown up responding to the world around us, influenced by our family, our friends (and enemies) and have adopted (successfully and unsuccessfully) to our environment. By the time we reached our respective career choices, we undergo training, which then introduces us to different dynamics. Making our emotions fit into these new environments can be difficult. Some acclimate well, and many others struggle. I know that I have worked on many different teams, including firefighters, security and law enforcement personnel, and in management teams as well.

Looking back, I find that in most cases I struggled to fit in, and this struggle impacted how to manage my emotions; thus, my behaviour. As I wrote earlier, I was a pushover, afraid of opening my mouth. I now know this came from a lack of confidence in myself. I believe I also wrote of my raging against the machine. I found my inability to control my frustration very disruptive. I am sure we have all been in the situation where we knew we were right, and for the right reason, and were refused. I recall in my early days of working in the security industry, I was hired into my very real team-based position. In this job, unfortunately, I learned that if I spoke up, I was either responded to with dismissal of my concerns or downright ridicule. I learned at that time to just go with the status quo, regardless that I have been told that this was a team environment.

It was this boss who told me not to worry about the things I could not control. I found that advice kind of clichéd at the time, but of course it was good advice in retrospect. I still struggled with this particular behaviour (and still do), but I was able to begin to incorporate this advice into my responses to stress. I also was finding that my lack of confidence was no longer appropriate, as I had begun my transformation process, and was now exploring my personality traits in the workplace.

I moved on to the company that I wrote about earlier , the one who refused to consider my contributions to grow the company. What I also brought to this employer was more of an outspoken and driven individual. I had decided to leave my comfort zone, and to put more risk into my career. Unfortunately, this was also an environment of deception and mistreatment. I also learned that, while being outspoken has its place in the

grand scheme of things, so does restraint. I found that my ideas and comments, while true and intended to improve things, were taken very critically and irked the people who managed me. As you may remember, I did not last very long at that job. However, I did come out of that experience with more skill in addressing changes in a more diplomatic manner. I took a risk, and unfortunately, it kind of blew up in my face; this was the first time I had ever been terminated from a job. Turns out it would not be the last.

What I was able to take away at this point in my career was the foundation of conflict management, the key of which was managing my emotions (zeal, anger, frustration) and standing up for what I believed was fair and right. I also had the opportunity to begin a path of training in the field of crisis management. This new me was recognized when I began working with a small start up security company. My interview was scheduled for thirty minutes, and I walked out after two hours, to a very not happy wife (who had been waiting for me). I was ecstatic that I had finally met a person who I connected with on a philosophical level and on a career trajectory in line with my own.

What I found was that I was in an environment that embraced what I had to
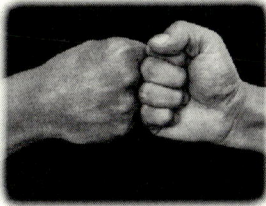 offer in its entirety. My stress levels dropped significantly, I was more motivated to exercise, and was able to flex my communication and conflict resolution muscles. When I faced conflict, I learned to talk things out. One of the other very valuable skills I developed (or instead of "skill" we will call it a personality trait) was empathy. Another was loyalty...
to the guy that set me up in the job that I ultimately learned the most out of all my jobs, before and since. Once again, there is an unfortunate coming...

It was during this time that I joined my local volunteer fire service. I had high hopes for the camaraderie that is supposed to be an
implicit aspect of small fire departments. Not so, as I discovered. While I was learning much about fire operations, I was also learning rather disappointingly, that egos are high, and teamwork and loyalty were not as fundamental as I thought it would be. Not that it was all negative, and I want to be clear here; I saw excellent examples of camaraderie, but I felt that I never truly fit in. I did not come out of the experience with any significant friendships, and I found that
there was much squabbling going on in the background, and more apparent on the fire ground than I could tolerate.

There was a cowboy on the team, and would always covet the tools on scene, leaving all unable to have practical experience. The cumulative experience was challenging on many levels, and when I consider the pain, suffering, and death I encountered, I left the department without a significant counterbalance of positive to offset the negative.

From that point, leading up to my first law enforcement position, I experienced nothing but organizational strife and conflict. I worked in environments where I experienced unethical and unprofessional behaviour.

I was an adult educator and was very excited to finally ascend to such a position, as it was my path of choice as the police career was starting to look like a dud. However, I encountered extreme compromise in the interest of the almighty dollar. When I first met my class, they were a hostile crowd. I discovered that they had been told an outright lie regarding the legitimacy and acceptance of the end credential. When I set the record straight, there was a mini revolt. I lost two students out of that class. There was much griping and toxicity, and much "How come the other classes ..." I finally had to apply a life lesson to my class, and in the process, solidified it into my own head. I told them that I would give them valuable tools to get into the industry and succeed. These skills would earn them valuable life and work experience that is sought by their chosen employers. I also told them to commit to the learning process and they would benefit as much as they put into it. I also counselled them that what other students in that campus did was none of their concern, nor was the wrong done to them by the organization.

I encouraged them to focus on the education that I could bestow upon them and take it for what it was worth. I assured them that the diploma was only one check in a box of many. Once the credential was on their walls, the real criteria they would be judged on would begin. I told them that I was not entirely pleased by the events leading up to this conflict, but that we all would have to get passed it and focus on why we were all there. It turned out successfully for the students. I was sure that this recipe would work for any other disgruntled students that came into my classroom. I also knew that I would need to involve myself in the admissions process to ensure the goals of the applicant were in line with my program.

Another example that still gets my blood pressure to rise is a staff member in a position of trust commit theft from a client. This incident was reported to me by her partner (who witnessed the incident), and I conducted my investigation, leading up to evidence of not only the original theft, but also the fraudulent cover-up after this person returned the item. I lobbied for the termination of this employee, as I also

uncovered that this was not the first recorded offence of this nature. I came up against the bargaining unit, and my own management folded like a tent (as this group was historically apt to do). I then lobbied for a two-week suspension, and again was informed it was too punitive. I was eventually successful in issuing a one-week suspension, much to my frustration. Did I mention that this person was in a position of trust? I left shortly thereafter for a week to attend a conference, and upon my return I discovered that the week suspension had been pared down to a one-day suspension. I was very disillusioned by this and was galled that the message to all my staff was that theft by them is tolerated. I then had to continue working with such a person on my staff.

I lobbied for the right course of action and had to come to grips with not getting my way, right or wrong. This was very typical of the environment at this place of employment. I had to learn that controlling my emotions was easier, because I got to the point of CYA (we all know what that means) and not caring beyond what I was able to accomplish for my staff.

Why am I telling these stories? I had to learn to control my emotions to an extent that I would not pass on my emotions to my students or staff. This was a very hard task for me to accomplish. It made me laugh the first time I watched the movie "Saving Private Ryan" and I watched the scene when Tom Hanks' character says to one of his non-commissioned ranks,

> *"I don't gripe to you, Reiben. I'm a captain. There's a chain of command. Gripes go up, not down. Always up. You gripe to me, I gripe to his superior officer, so on, so on, and so on. I don't gripe to you. I don't gripe in front of you. You should know that as a Ranger."*

It was a struggle for me, because I wanted to show my staff that I was not blind; that I saw what they saw and felt what they felt. I recall during one staff meeting that I delivered the same speech I had given my class of students earlier. Focus on your role and do not concern yourself with the gripes of others. We will see later in the book the effect of toxic people on group dynamics, but these are examples of how not to become the toxic contaminant in your group, especially when you are in a role of command.

I wrote earlier about my mama bear boss. I went from that environment, a very small team, to a larger organization and a larger team. I found the transition to be very rough; in the process stepping on a lot of toes, went beyond boundaries I had not had to deal with previously, and ruffled the feathers of my direct teammates. Unfortunately, this also coincided with my rapidly declining mental state, which certainly did not make things any easier. The problem here is that, with mama bear, I felt free to express the real me, and to unequivocally state my opinions without fear of conflict. She would call BS when she thought it was appropriate or listened intently until I had fully explained my intentions or my activity. In my new environment, this was completely opposite. I encountered very sensitive people, and my sense of humour was less than welcome. I tried to stay true to myself and to unburden myself very candidly with my boss. In some ways, this helped. In many ways, it did not; especially due to our very different personalities and styles of managing conflict. I was given a picture prior to being hired about this environment, and for a variety of reasons, the picture was not as accurately painted as I was made to believe.

I learned a very foundational lesson about courage fairly late in life that shook me to my core. I'm never very hesitant to enter a fray while I am on duty, in full uniform and with full authority to do what I do. One summer, a situation occurred in which I had an opportunity to intervene in a situation, and I hesitated. A child was being physically abused by an angry parent in public, and it is still very difficult for me to admit that I did not do anything to intervene. It is, however, important to note that I was not on duty at the time. While I think I know the reason why I didn't actively respond, I'm not happy with these reasons. So, I want to write about the way that we make up our minds to face certain fears... certain hesitations, that we have in life when it comes to facing conflict. This idea came to me to write about this upon sitting down and doing a "10 Things You May Not Know About Me" game on social media. The first thing I wrote is that I am extremely shy and non-confrontational by nature. I think about this situation quite often and must deal with, to be perfectly honest, the shame that I feel and the utter disappointment in myself, considering the parties involved in the situation.

I think it's important to understand ourselves, and why we do the things we do, in order to understand the things we do, and thus prompting us to change the things that we will do in the future. As I am not perfect, I try to do this quite often, and I have had a lot of difficulty in dealing with this situation. I suspect that I always will.

Ultimately what I must come to terms with is that I was afraid to do anything for a reason I believe was based upon that non-confrontational trait. I was afraid of what I might end up having to do. As a law enforcement officer, I have certain authorities to intervene in certain things, and ultimately to arrest a person. This uncertainty was even more exacerbated by the fact that I was not on duty, nor was I in uniform, nor was I in my marked patrol vehicle when this situation occurred. I hesitated to intervene in the situation because I think I may have been afraid of having to pursue avenues that may have potentially gotten me into trouble, even though I know, personally and professionally, that I would have been lawfully placed, to do what needed to be done. However, this situation involved children, a large group of the public, we were far from a timely police response, and my family was present. I may have been so hesitant because, as a civilian as I was that day, I did not clearly carry my authority on my sleeve, so to speak. Additionally, I perhaps was concerned with the volatility of the situation, and that the situation may have led to a physical altercation. I could not rely on the clear and present authority that I have when in uniform. So, I'm not entirely certain as to the strength of those reasons, or perhaps I was just afraid to intervene.

However, justifications aside, what I do know is that it has prompted me to give significant consideration to my self-concept. I always thought of myself as the protector, I have always acted like I was the protector and it is something that has contributed to my self-concept: who I think I am and who other people think I am. I view this as a complete and utter failure on my part to fulfill that role of protector. I think it is important for us, regardless if you are in the law enforcement profession or any other first responder agency, to give some sincere consideration as to how you develop your self concepts.

Additionally, it's important to ensure that we do not come to a screeching, grinding halt whenever we do or do not do something that is completely out of character involving something that we consider foundational to who we are. Something like that can utterly shatter one's confidence, and I consider myself to be one of the most confident people out there, even considering my shyness and my non-confrontational manner. As such, here are some things to think about: are we willing and are we able to go to the extreme lengths it may perhaps take us when we encounter a situation that we are not prepared? Or how about being prepared emotionally or not being in a professional frame of mind to deal with? Or, more importantly, when we are not actively thinking or ready in our minds to deal with the scenario that suddenly presents itself with little time to actual give it some thought.

One of the people I quote often and that I consider a very significant foundation builder for me is Lt. Col. Dave Grossman. Two of my favourite and influential quotes that I've used and will continue to use throughout my life may apply here. First, "You do not rise to the occasion, you sink to your training." But remember, as I said, this situation did not involve my professional mindset, it did not involve me being at work, and it did not involve even my training. The second quote is that "You are only as sick as your secrets." This quote involves one of the reasons why I'm finally writing of this situation. Now this is not exactly a secret, as my wife and I have discussed this situation at length, but until now, it is not a situation that I have shared publicly. I do not want to be sick, and I especially do not want to be sick with this secret. I think that these thoughts permeate all my life lessons that I write about. Perhaps this story can be useful in determining your own life lessons.

When we address any level of change, or management of the self, we all have a wide variety of de-railers: those behaviours and thoughts that remove us from the track of accomplishing a specific goal we have set for ourselves. Just as a tiny flaw in the track can derail a train, simple negativity can send us careening off our paths. The Arbinger Institute, an organization with the mandate to increase awareness of the pervasive issue of self-deception in leadership and speaks of the two de-railers of self-deception and self-betrayal. In their book, *Leadership and Self-Deception* (2010)[13], they describe self-deception as being in a box. Generally, they mirror the analogy of think outside the box, except that it is not just our thinking process that is boxed in. It is us entirely. Basically, when we are not open to learning something new, acclimating to something new, or opening ourselves to acknowledge a new truth, we enter the box. While they generally apply the self-deception and betrayal to an organizational setting, I feel it is applicable to self-development of anyone.

This can become somewhat of a chicken and the egg scenario, in that did things go sour because we were in the box, or was it things going sour that put us in the box? I like to think that it does not matter. I am hoping that you can work yourself out of your box regardless of how you entered it. I further believe that we are all in a box to some degree. First responders typically end up in stronger, more secure boxes due to the social, occupational, organizational and self-imposed pressures. Ultimately, this approach describes how we get into the box and then make others around us enter their own. The point here is that it is not just you being affected by your isolation and boxing yourself up.

Self-betrayal occurs when I act contrary to what I feel I should do for another. So, for what ever reason, we experience embarrassment or shame. We all make mistakes, but if we are not highly self aware and if we cannot control our emotions, we will likely hide from the truth of our own misdeeds. This can lead to moral injuries, and these can be very difficult to overcome.

When I betray myself, I begin to see the world in a way that justifies my self-betrayal. In effect, I start projecting my failures and weaknesses onto the people around me. I worked with a person who did this on a regular basis.

---

[13] *Leadership and Self- Deception*, (2010), The Arbinger Institute, Berrett-Koehler Publishers Inc. San Francisco, CA

Whenever he was caught doing something wrong, he would invariably respond, "But Dean does it.", regardless of the truth of it. The only way we can live with our failures is to drag everyone else down to our level, so we can justify our actions now that everyone else wallows down here with us.

When I see the world in a self-justifying way, my view of reality becomes distorted. Typically, we see that in the crusty veteran first responder. Because we see the worst of society, both in people and events, we experience the reality that most others do not. Unfortunately, that reality that we see does not necessarily reflect reality in general, only the reality in the small area of it that we experience. Because we see the same people repeatedly in crisis, and because we face the same abuses repeatedly, and because we experience the same unreasonable demands, we tend to evolve into seeing these qualities in society. I think we all know deep down that society, in fact, is not reflected accurately based upon these narrow experiences. It just gets too hard to fight the fight to maintain a positive view of the world around us.

This situation refers to one in which I failed to act in line with all that I believe I am and is the only issue in my life that I will classify as a moral injury. It is an anchor to my otherwise buoyant confidence in myself. Feel free to backtrack and take a read. I swore that I would never fail to stand up and do the hard job. I faced that very same challenge recently, and I struggled to make the hard decision, but this time, I did the hard job and may just have possibly saved a couple kids from an unhealthy environment and hopefully provided a family with the resources out there available to help families in strife. I can at least look into the mirror once again and have some sense that I'm capable of not being a complete hypocrite.

These self-deceptions create a self-betrayal rich environment. When we betray ourselves to believe in things that are not true, regardless of the reason, we enter the box. In the box, we isolate ourselves, and not physically. We insulate ourselves from the truth. We can no longer hear outside influences, we cannot see outside stimuli; we are literally stuck with ourselves, and by nature of being isolated, we are less likely to be open to positive change. Even if we are not completely encased in that box, we can compartmentalize our personalities and carry numerous boxes that are created in the same manner. Over time, certain boxes become characteristic of us, and we carry them with us day to day, place to place.

This becomes a toxicity to our teams. Being boxed is not just an individual problem. By being in the box, I provoke others to be in their own boxes. We all have the potential to undergo this transformation, and when boxing occurs in a team environment, nothing but conflict and co-dependence results. In the box, we invite mutual mistreatment and obtain mutual justification. We collude in giving each other reason to stay in the box.

Naturally, after discussing becoming toxic, now we will address detoxing ourselves. Detoxifying ourselves and our teams will not be as easy as a shot of naloxone either. It is more akin to undergoing long-term treatment. It takes much introspection, soul searching, and possibly some pain and fear. It also includes taking risks on behalf of our mental health and opening the lines of communication so that we may divest ourselves of our demons, deceptions and betrayals.

We must also consider the contagion effect of toxic team environments. It is common knowledge that negativity is catching, no different than colds. Just as germs are spread by coughing and sneezing, our negative thoughts are spread by opening our mouths, and then support what is coming out of our mouths with our behaviours.

CHAPTER 9

Nailing Down the Rug: The Necessity of Support

We all have our own personal styles when it comes to coping. We will speak to the importance of accurately assessing the effectiveness and healthiness of these styles. Maladaptive coping and effective coping will be discussed. We cannot necessarily count on organizational support; and as Ian's story demonstrates, we must be prepared for the rug to be whipped out from underneath us at any time. Although John was fortunate that he received the support we would expect from our employers, as in the case of Ian, we cannot expect that our organizations will support us in our darkest moments.

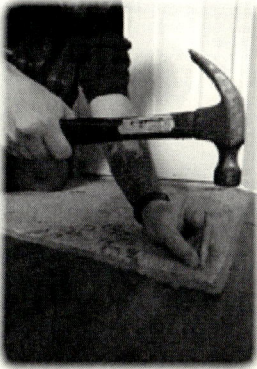

Keith Ferazzi[14] "Who's Got Your Back": lifeline as a personal success principle primarily in a business setting. However, why cannot these "People" serve the same way in mental health rescue endeavours? Lifeline relationships are critical. A lifeline relationship is one between equals, between peers, between individuals who can be intellectually and emotional sparring partners and confidants. If you find yourself struggling, out of balance, and want to seek coherence, reach out! Self reflection and striving to make necessary changes is valuable but know that if you encounter a path that you do not and cannot recognize the landmarks, find someone who can shed some light in the unfamiliar.

Years ago, I wrote in a blog about *karma*. In it, I told a story from my days working in a transitional housing facility (homeless shelter). I present it here for you to illustrate truly how powerful life lines can be when created by treating people with kindness, respect and sincerity. I have seen my good deeds come back to support me when I really needed someone backing me.

---

[14] Ferrazzi, K. (2009), *Who's Got Your Back*, Random House Inc. New York, New York

The most telling example of karma in my career occurred after developing a very positive rapport with a prolific homeless man while working a security post at the shelter. He called himself "Dog". My partner and I spoke on many occasions with this man and attempted to help him overcome some of his challenges, but generally just chatted with him. To be candid, my partner was

an attractive woman, which is why I think Dog began hanging around us. However, through informal chatting, we discovered that he had spent time in prison for a violent crime (reason is immaterial), and that he was currently facing assault charges in an unrelated situation. Our staff had already encountered his challenging behaviour but dealt with it in more of an aggressive approach. Since we were calm and more interpersonal with him, Dog spoke of his anger issues and his struggles as a homeless man. We tried to counsel Dog, giving him some strategies to help him work out his issues, and he seemed open to them. He was concerned that he would be returned to prison when his assault charges were heard. We had developed a connection with him, one that would provide much needed support down the road.

Shortly thereafter, during a difficult arrest, my co-worker and her new partner were being assaulted by a second party, Dog appeared and put his street credibility and ultimately his own safety on the line to defend a security guard (the enemy), by physically forcing the removal of the arrestee's friend from the area... right in front of his peers. If you have worked or know anything about the street lifestyle and environment, you can grasp the significance of this act. I seriously think that, had we not developed a rapport with the man, and had we not treated him as a human being, this story might have a different ending.

One of the more significant connections I made when working on my issues was being tagged in a Facebook challenge called the Twenty-Two Push-Up Challenge. The premise was that, statistically, twenty-two first responders take their own lives every day. I decided to add a reflection to each photo of my push-ups for each day's output. It made me reflect daily on the issues that can lead to first responder suicide. They are just as pertinent now than back then, so I will share them here.

Day 1

Daily Reflection: I have and still manage some of my own emotional issues that I believe are the result of my occupation. I also know several first responders that have fought very private battles. So, to raise awareness, I will do twenty-two push-ups every day for twenty-two days—that is the pledge.

Day 2

Daily Reflection: I struggled today with the pain of doing my push-ups due to being horribly stiff from yesterday's. Very appropriate comparison to struggling with anxiety and sometimes it gets harder after the initial effort to address it.

Day 3

Daily Reflection: When I do these, I curse it because I'm not a fan of pain and after 3 days of physical pain, I am reminded that what I'm feeling is a minor inconvenience compared to what suffering our first responders go through.

Day 4

Daily Reflection: I could quit this challenge due to my discomfort with stiff muscles, but those suffering from occupational emotional trauma do not have that choice. So, I will not wuss out and will stick through it.

Day 5

Daily Reflection: I decided to do today's push-ups in the dark. My intention is to show my friends how in the dark most people are regarding occupational emotional trauma. As well, to show how sufferers feel in that they believe no one understands.

Day 6

Daily Reflection: we are really not alone in this world, and those closest, both in proximity and emotional connection, are our families. My youngest daughter chose to share the experience with her old man.

Day 7

Daily Reflection: we really cannot move forward with treatment until we can look ourselves in the face and admit there is a problem. As such, I did my twenty-two push-ups looking at this guy in the face.

Day 8

Daily Reflection: While I had no *daily reflection* for this day, I specifically asked my lovely wife to help me demonstrate that spousal/significant other support is vital. It also shows that, even after all the rocky years, she has not abandoned me. I love her for it!

Day 9

Daily Reflection: after doing my push-ups on gravel and concrete in full duty gear as the mosquitoes swarm me. It's a true reflection of the weight of the office of first responder, and a true reflection of the unimportant things literally swarming you and draining your very life's blood.

Day 10

Daily Reflection: we may face our issues down in the dirt, so today I did my push-ups down in the dirt.

Day 11

Daily Reflection: I have no reflection... just a guy doing push-ups.

Day 12

Daily Reflection: the stresses and pains we suffer come with us everywhere we go, even to a place of fun and happiness like an amusement park.

Day 13

Daily Reflection: for traffic enforcement, I am issued a hi-vis (high visibility) vest, the very one I am wearing during my push-ups today. We have this tool so people can see the hazard, and it makes people more aware to deal with our presence in a manner that protects our bodies. Unfortunately, we are not given such a tool to recognize the mental and emotional struggles. There is no hi-vis vest for what is going on in our

heads. If you are suffering, hi-vis it by telling someone. If you are friend or family with a first responder, hi-vis it by becoming familiar with the signs of stress and be on the look-out. Hi-vis is about awareness, and so is this challenge. Secondary reflection: push-ups in full duty uniform blows, doing push-ups on gravel blows, and mosquitoes blow!

Day 14

Daily Reflection: mental health issues are very difficult to see day to day. Most of our aberrant feelings are hidden, as most of me is hidden in the grass. And the feeling of being stuck in a rut is just as hidden, as I am doing my push-ups virtually hidden in a roadside ditch.

Day 15

Daily Reflection: just a guy doing push-ups. However, looking back on this photo, I think it shows how fuzzy and blurry our reality can become when in the grip of our mental conditions.

Day 16

Daily Reflection: ever since my mental health issues began, I have been constantly asked if I use exercise as a way to deal with my stress. This is where I say Hell No! So, since this challenge is about awareness and overcoming post-traumatic stress disorder, I've decided to up my push-ups from twenty-two to twenty-five. I intend to keep working my way up from there.

Day 17

Daily Reflection: why not do my twenty-five push-ups surrounded by my dogs? My buddies are with me!

Day 18

Daily Reflection: even with dealing with our day to day challenges, it's important to know that we can, in fact, accomplish and build things. I figured that, today, I would do my twenty-five push-ups in the beautiful sunshine with my weekend accomplishments in the background... gates that I have been putting off for two years. Accomplished!

Day 19

Daily Reflection: other than upping my push-ups from twenty-two to twenty-five and today's thirty, I have nothing special about this day's part of the challenge. Just got finished cleaning the garage, so I didn't care to get dressed again, so I am hiding from the camera! I cannot remember last when I could do thirty push-ups in a row.

Day 20

Daily Reflection: no reflection today about my push-ups except that my wall gecko is always looking out over me! Considering the comfort of my room with familiar things, our creature comforts play a role in maintaining positive moods.

Day 21

Daily Reflection: how can you let your anxieties ruin the experience of being in such a majestic place? I will not today! Doing push-ups in a National Park!

Day 22

Daily Reflection: it takes effort to get above your mental health issues, whatever they are. It just takes effort, but the view when you get there is worth the effort! And again, my daughter joined me.

10

CHAPTER

Final Thoughts

Ultimately, what I see is that, while I'm not as much around the bend as I thought, there is much that I can do to further my journey into self development. There should be no stigma attached to seeking out help when one finds oneself on an unfamiliar path. I just want to have coherence. Coherence between my mind, my heart and my emotions. I've always been led by my mind and heart; it just seems that now in my recent past and present, my emotions seem to be in charge.

Just because some of us do not suffer from post-traumatic stress disorder, our traumatic experiences have a cumulative effect and lead to very real psychological disorders and conditions. I have been professionally involved in over a dozen fatalities in my career, and have attended or experienced other trauma throughout my career (and that doesn't even compare to most of my colleagues). Even if you feel they do not affect you, believe me, they do. And that is coming from a guy who effectively managed to suppress all these stressors for over twenty years.

Do not dismiss the reality of vicarious trauma; it is a very real thing. Your own traumatic experiences soften you up and make you very susceptible to reacting adversely to others' trauma, even to such a degree where you aren't even personally involved in the traumatic event. On the flip side, your trauma can very much traumatize those around you. This is not to say that communicating with your friends and family outside of the first responder community will be detrimental, but just be sensitive of that fact.

Grow Pride: I have found that I have spiralled into a vortex of negativity (ironic since I was so satisfied with my new environment), and it has been aggravated by my mental health conditions, and it is one that I am making a pledge to myself to win the battle. I am going to work on my pride in what

I do. I know that I can hold my head up high knowing that I am part of an honourable, demanding, complex, challenging and rewarding profession. I have chosen to serve my community as a law enforcement professional. I will continue to have pride in the uniform I wear and the badge I carry because of what they represent. I will take pride in the reality that my community is safer because I have chosen to serve.

Grow Courage: I will continue to grow the courage to do what is right even when it is not what is popular or what is expedient. Although I will change how I will challenge the things that have grown my negativity, I will continue to embrace the courage to address life threatening or negative behaviour with my peers. As always, I will continue to embrace the courage to stand up and own up when I make a mistake and move forward better off for the experience.

Grow Leadership: I have failed to follow my own path and that of which I preach in fostering a culture of leadership in my life and my agency by falling victim to my own negativity. I will focus more so to teach and model leadership at all levels of my organization and within the community, and through my business interests. I am fortunate to work on a team that fosters leadership all around, and I will work on doing my part.

Grow Personally: I have made many changes over my life, some due to necessity, some just because I wanted to. Brian Willis talks of growing personally by choosing to invest in your personal growth. Although I feel I'm perfect now, my wife and children will probably disagree. So, for that, I am willing to keep going on the personal change wagon! There's so much out there, not necessarily to learn, *per se*, but to consider. I have also reluctantly accepted that I need to invest in my fitness and health. Getting old is not fun, physically AND mentally! But considering my advancing age, my pre-existing health concerns, it's better to be prepared to survive mental health stressors. Continue to embrace all training that you can get.

Grow Professionally: With the plethora of information regarding first responder mental health and the in-service training slowly becoming available, take advantage to learn as much as you can, both about yourself and your brother and sister first responders. I, for one, will continue to take advantage of any training that will inevitably come my way.

Grow Relationships: All the changes I have made in my career were made with the support of my loving wife. My wife has been a rock in my life (acting at times as an anchor, proverbial ball and chain sometimes, and valuable cornerstone at other times). She has held me back (necessary), slowed me down (necessary), and supported me in times of uncertainty and risk. And my children sacrificed without any control over what happened to them, but went along without self-destructing. Family is vital for me, and all of what I've pursued has had them in mind, including their well-being, their future, and their character. I have always been shy, and it is difficult internally for me to step out of my comfort zone as it pertains to creating new relationships. I have done a lot of stepping out over the more recent years, and it has not killed me, so I am considering expanding my involvement in many ways. One thing has made itself clear: we have surrounded ourselves with people that have done us well. Relationships are key to life, both personally and professionally. We have been blessed by the friends and colleagues that necessitate success, we just need to acknowledge and celebrate it.

Grow the Next Generation: Commit to growing the next generation of first responder professionals by embracing the positives they bring to the profession, by being more intentional about mentoring, taking time to listen and to allow them to teach you. I have always embraced these principles during my years of training and teaching. However, I find that I have failed to keep my negativity to myself, and clothed it in the garb of "reality" during conversations with peers, convincing myself that this was in the interest of giving them the full story. This, again, flies in the face of my personal leadership development and ethics. We need to make sure that our own negativity does not tarnish their own abilities to critically analyze the goings-on in the world, especially when recent events may cause them concern for the safety of their teammates and selves.

Be proactive! Don't wait for a person who loves you so very much to have to throw you under the bus with your health care professional. Not only can we get valuable advice about ourselves from our lifelines, people around us can provide encouragement when we begin to experience that beat-down.

Be in charge! You matter, and you are the only one who can put you in a position to stabilize yourself and get better. Be an active participant in facing your stressors.

Be vocal! Talk to peers, colleagues, family, professionals, whoever can provide much needed support. Don't give in, don't cave. It's very hard to motivate yourself when in a depressive state, I know. I truly know. All I wanted to do was sleep when I got home from work tonight. I made myself take my dog for a romp in the snow and then finally sit down and get this blog out.

Be educated! There are so many resources out there. Read books. Internet research. Reach out to people and organizations that might be able to provide info. Go to courses, seminars, professional development:

Be safe! If you feel like you are going to hurt yourself, give yourself at least an hour and then yell... scream... holler for help!

Look to others for guidance! We all know how to manoeuvre in our homes in the dark due to the familiarity of our floor plans, but every now and again, we stub our toes on something. Sometimes, we just need ambient light to get through. Our lifelines are that light. We all have lifelines out there, but if you don't... get one or two. However, I think most of us would be surprised that, if we think we don't have any, there really are people in our lives that will provide us with candid assessments of ourselves and our situations. At the least, these people can be sounding boards for venting without judgment, and at the most, they will have a perspective that will help light the path. However, for this to be truly effective, you must see #1 and be prepared to be honest with yourself and your lifeline for the interaction to bear fruit. If you are truly blessed with a multitude of lifelines, then seek them out in a manner that puts the right person in the conversation who may provide the most benefit to your issue. Beware that you are not strictly seeking validation of your own thoughts. Remember, honesty is the key when working within ourselves. Seek out lifelines that will challenge your current perspective.

Be active in your own self development! Sometimes you cannot see the forest through the trees, and neither can those close to you. I don't expect anyone to just look in the mirror, think for a while, and come up with the answers. I certainly haven't. But what I did do was start reading. For some, like me, reading anything non-fiction is a chore. And you may have to read LOTS of books to find the those that resonate with you specifically. But it lends outside perspectives that may be completely foreign to your thinking, and provide a broader way of seeing your self, your behaviour, your environment, and those around you. And I have a bookshelf and tablet FULL of books in this vein, and I've learned crazy amounts that I would otherwise not have considered. Some are crap, some are gems! In many of these resources, you can find both things that it's not, as well as some that are, contributing factors to your stress.

Understand that there ARE some things in life that cause us stress that we truly cannot control. The challenge becomes adapting to the environment. We have options... always. The trap, however, is developing a sense of what's called learned helplessness. Learned helplessness occurs when we, following sustained stressors and continued loss of control over the situation, finally give in and give up. Unfortunately, this deadening we feel inside is neither productive nor a reduction of stress. It is just the opposite. It leads to classic avoidance behaviour, which just prolongs and/or delays the issue. This issue will eventually have to be dealt with, and it does not just go away, as I have found lately with my own stressors. The culmination of mine have all come back to roost, and are now manifesting themselves not only psychologically, but physiologically as well. Not healthy at all!

To sum up, pledge to yourself that you will look honestly within, and that you will look outside for helpful perspectives, to research, to be active in your growth, and strive not to batter yourself against that which you cannot control. Stress is a reality, but so is our ability to effectively combat it.

Need help? Get help.

Cheers.
Dean Young
February 2018